MW00974181

Savoring SINGLE

SHELLEY BLACK

WESTBOW
PRESS®
A DIVISION OF THOMAS NELSON
& ZONDERVAN

Copyright © 2017 Shelley Black.

All rights reserved. No part of this book may be used or reproduced by any means, graphic, electronic, or mechanical, including photocopying, recording, taping or by any information storage retrieval system without the written permission of the author except in the case of brief quotations embodied in critical articles and reviews.

This book is a work of non-fiction. Unless otherwise noted, the author and the publisher make no explicit guarantees as to the accuracy of the information contained in this book and in some cases, names of people and places have been altered to protect their privacy.

Scripture quotations are taken from the Holy Bible, New Living Translation, copyright ©1996, 2004, 2007, 2013, 2015 by Tyndale House Foundation. Used by permission of Tyndale House Publishers, Inc., Carol Stream, Illinois 60188. All rights reserved.

Scripture quotations marked TPT are taken from The Passion Translation TM, copyright © 2012, 2013, 2014, 2015. Used by permission of 5 Fold Media, LLC, Syracuse, NY 13039, United States of America. All rights reserved. Unless otherwise indicated.

Unless otherwise indicated, all Scripture quotations are taken from THE MESSAGE, copyright © 1993, 1994, 1995, 1996, 2000, 2001, 2002 by Eugene H. Peterson. Used by permission of NavPress. All rights reserved. Represented by Tyndale House Publishers, Inc.

Scripture quotations taken from the New American Standard Bible® (NASB), Copyright © 1960, 1962, 1963, 1968, 1971, 1972, 1973, 1975, 1977, 1995 by The Lockman Foundation Used by permission.

WestBow Press books may be ordered through booksellers or by contacting:

WestBow Press
A Division of Thomas Nelson & Zondervan
1663 Liberty Drive
Bloomington, IN 47403
www.westbowpress.com
1 (866) 928-1240

Because of the dynamic nature of the Internet, any web addresses or links contained in this book may have changed since publication and may no longer be valid. The views expressed in this work are solely those of the author and do not necessarily reflect the views of the publisher, and the publisher hereby disclaims any responsibility for them.

Any people depicted in stock imagery provided by Thinkstock are models, and such images are being used for illustrative purposes only. Certain stock imagery © Thinkstock.

ISBN: 978-1-9736-1059-5 (sc)
ISBN: 978-1-9736-1060-1 (hc)
ISBN: 978-1-9736-1058-8 (e)

Library of Congress Control Number: 2017918070

Print information available on the last page.

WestBow Press rev. date: 11/22/2017

"Savor"
[sey-ver]

to give oneself to the enjoyment of

Dictionary.com

Contents

Devotions

Foreword

I sign off on all of my blogs by saying, "in this with you girl." When you read through to the end of this book, it's closed the same way. Even from the beginning of how Savoring Single unfolded, I realized how much of what I shared, God was still working in me.

It also comes from a place of having likely walked a very similar path to yours. I grew up playing with Barbies and dolls, convinced I'd have my own love story and family in my early twenties.

When all those years came and went and still no dream come true, I probably had the same thoughts you've had. Believed the same lies the enemy has told you. Felt similar grief, not by loss, but spending "my best years" without the one thing I wanted the most.

I have sat in that same dark room wondering why my life didn't seem to matter. Cried the same tears as realities became too hard to bear alone, but having no shoulder to lean on, because I was. Alone.

This book isn't because I did it all right, and isn't because my life is perfect now. The only reason I have anything to offer is because God pursued me as I ran, kept speaking even when I ignored Him, loved me when I was unlovable and hasn't changed a single one of His promises over my life.

In my heart, I still desire to get married one day. It's just that now my heart is wrapped in the arms of my loving Father who whispers to my longing, "I've got you. It's going to be okay."

I figured by now I wouldn't deal with the same things I used to, but that's really just an unrealistic expectation. I still do. I still see proposals on Instagram and long for my own. I still get asked why I haven't gotten married yet. When I run into friends from back in the day, I still wish I could tell them who I married. And still fight the temptation to be ashamed that I can't.

The circumstances of being single haven't changed. But I do respond different, now. My self-talk uses different words. Depression doesn't visit me anymore and despair no longer stays for the night.

I am truly *in this with you girl*. Still single. Still desiring to one day be married. Still loving Jesus and wanting to live a life that pleases Him. Since you are reading this, I have a feeling this may be how you feel, too. So just know, that we're in this together.

Introduction

Hey girl,

I am thrilled that this book has made it into your hands!

So…you're single, huh? Me too. At least we're in this together. And I've got a feeling that there's a whole bunch of us feeling pretty close to the same way as we journey through what it means to be single.

For me, coming to terms with my singleness has taken a long time. I fought it, denied it, tried to run from it. I finally faced it and, so far, it hasn't been so bad. I've learned a ton about who I am. I've also really gotten to know the heart of my Father God through the process. That alone has been well worth the journey! I hope this book unfolds a better way for you and, hopefully, will save you some of the heartache and pain, disappointment and loss that I have experienced.

Why Savoring Single? Because if we idolize another season, we will be blind to the importance of the one we are in. If we think our best is ahead of us in marriage, career or success or even behind us in memories of days gone by or that time when everything seemed perfect, we will miss the treasure of our todays. You have such a treasure in this moment, that you won't have in the next. Enjoy life from this place, experience it from this perspective, appreciate the view from this point. There are so many amazing things to pull out of this time. So savor it!

I want to pray for you, so that as you read this book, God will speak in a special way that will impact your heart and this season of your life's journey.

Dear Abba Father,

Thank you for your wrap-around presence and your all-consuming love. Be with my girl as she reads these pages and speak to her between the lines about how you see her. I pray that her ears would be open and her heart responsive so that as You speak, she'll take the time to unfold the treasures you have waiting for her. You already know how special she is, so please help her see herself like you do. Thank You that you are leading her on a journey with you that will mend her heart, even in areas she may not realize she's hurting. I pray you bring peace to the storm of her soul that has allowed lies to trouble the waters for far too long. You are her hope, her love, her peace, her life. Rewrite her story with the pen of your love and redefine in her Your purpose. You have the most careful and tender hands of a master surgeon that leaves no scars, so take out old mindsets, uproot lies and untangle the web of culture's influence on her heart. I ask that You would then seal her again with Your embrace as You call her by name into oneness with You. You are simply too good for words. Thank You.

In this with you, girl!

Shelley

Chapter One: Finally Facing Single

I flew on my first airplane when I was eight years old. Alone. Yes, you read that right. Alone. Granted, it was in the early nineties when flying regulations were much simpler and the world felt like a safer place. My parents checked me in for my flight and walked me all the way to the gate where I boarded the plane. I was headed to visit my BFF, who had moved out of state, and my age didn't seem like any big deal at the time.

I wasn't nervous at all. My sister bought me a bag full of candy and the sweetest advice to chew gum during take-off and landing. She assured me that the gum would help keep my ears from popping. I wasn't even sure what that meant, but was happy for the free candy. I packed my Peter Pan sleeping bag, a diary, a pair of denim shorts covered in daisies, and with a full bag of candy in hand, I flew into the first of many adventures, alone.

Not only was I not nervous, I also didn't realize I was alone. I left the loving embrace of parents in one state only to be welcomed into the comfort of friendship in another. The two-and-a-half-hour direct flight in between felt like only minutes. The adventure was exhilarating. There I sat with my very own bag of peanuts, pillow and blanket, all provided by the airline. I soaked up every last drop of wonder, recirculated air and Sprite while I spent those few hours gleaming, as I watched out my window at the world below.

This scenario has played out a hundred times over in my life. Of course, I wasn't eight years old for all of them, but have been on many adventures, traveled across the globe, soaked up wonder and headed fearlessly into the unknown. And many of these times, I have been alone.

Alone didn't feel like a bad thing until I hit middle school. As a kid, it all felt like it was just part of the adventure. But then it became something I couldn't just overlook as normal. As I grew even older, I saw other friends having similar adventures, now sprinkled in with new ones like boyfriends, engagements, beautiful weddings and children.

In light of these, my adventures seemed to fade in comparison to the seasons of life they were already living. Life seemed to lose a bit of color like the photo filters that mimic vintage photography. They're fun as an option but lose their appeal when your whole life seems to become colorless and flat.

Hills and Valleys..

The journey of life is filled with hills and valleys. I've had high seasons and some pretty low ones. You probably have too. It was in those valleys that most of my days seemed dark, sad and lonely. Because I felt alone, I looked to myself as the one to blame for my singleness, as though I had messed up God's plan for my life. When those excuses ran dry I began to blame God. I felt like He had rejected me. I believed that I wasn't good enough to marry one of His sons and that my singleness was proof of my unworthiness. This contradicted the belief in my heart, so when it became hard to blame God, I blamed my local church. It was small and lacked eligible bachelors. The list goes on and on. So did the days, months and years of living life lack luster with an overlay of disappointment and thoroughly convinced that I was missing out. Here's a story about a valley, a pit actually, one you may feel like you're in right now.

> "One day, a donkey fell into a pit. The animal cried and whined for hours while his owner tried to figure out what to do. Finally, the farmer decided that since the animal was old, and the pit needed to be covered up anyway, he'd just bury the old donkey right there. He got a shovel and started filling in the pit… At first, when the donkey realized what was happening, he cried even more piteously. But then the wise animal hit on a plan. As each spadeful of dirt hit his back, the donkey would shake it off and take a step up on the growing mound of earth. Eventually, the mound grew high enough for him to jump out of the pit."

> Jewish Parable "The Donkey in the Pit" by Yaakov Lieder

Maybe you are like the donkey that has already fallen into the pit. When life seems hopeless and unchanging, our hearts cry out from the pain of heartache. I know what it means to feel the physical pain of loneliness. The best advice, words of encouragement and love from even our dearest friends and family, can seem inadequate to the reality of our situation. You may even be reading this book unsure if it will really help. My hope is that as you read, it will be like shovels of dirt enabling you to climb out.

I'd like to point out that the donkey had two choices. Had he given up hope, the farmer's efforts would have buried him. If you are already in the valley, in the pit, being covered by the dirt of years still single, not dating and feeling unloved, I encourage you to shake it off once more. Begin taking steps to shift the perspective of your heart to hope again. This farmer may have decided the donkey was too old but God has not given up on you. Those shovels of dirt are constant reminders of His love for you. He wants you. He's still working on your behalf.

Or maybe single didn't feel quite as obvious as it does now. Being single might have just seemed like a bi-product of a busy school schedule, balancing classes along with a job or sports team, or maybe friendships having been your priority. As seasons of life change, friends and schedules will too. If you fall into the negative cycles concerning your singleness it may lead to pity parties, raw emotions, sad days, lonely nights and a filter of disappointment even on things you once enjoyed.

My hope is that as you read this book, it will silence the doubt and fear about your single season and provide you with a more solid foundation so that the pit is filled in before you ever fall into it. You can walk between hilltops of being loved without experiencing the despair in between. That doesn't mean life is going to be perfect or that you will never feel lonely, but your perspective will fill in the gap and keep it from getting dangerously deep. More about this in the next chapter.

Being Single is Okay

I have learned that being single is okay. It doesn't mean that something is wrong with me, that I missed my opportunity or that God is punishing me in some way. Being single is simply a part of life. How I live that life, however high or low, is completely up to me.

From Dictionary.com, to savor is "to give yourself to the enjoyment of something." So, give yourself to enjoying single! It's a part of life and can be so much more enjoyable if we see it from a fuller perspective, living it out from the hilltop full of love, life and adventure. That's how you savor it!

So be encouraged because being single is actually a good thing. I know that's contrary to a lot of other voices out there, and we'll talk more about that later, but if you try to avoid being single or rush through it, you'll miss everything God wanted to develop in you through this once-in-a-lifetime part of your journey! There is a purpose for it and it likely won't last forever.

Our Need...

Just as much as it is okay to be single, it is okay to desire being loved, wanted, cherished and known. These are legitimate needs that are foundational to our lives as humans. Our culture has taught us that these are mostly met by friendships and dating relationships. This is true but only in part. Good, healthy, thriving relationships will enhance your life. God created you for relationships and desires your life to be full in every area! We see this from the beginning in the first mention of relationships in Scripture, "It is not good for the man to be alone. I will make a helper who is just right for him." Genesis 2:19 NLT

God saw Adam's need for a wife, but before He created Eve as a perfect match for him, God and Adam cultivated relationship together. You'll likely get married one day but it is important to understand that friends and boyfriends, or even your one-day husband, will never be able to completely satisfy your deepest need. God created you with a desire for relationship so you would always hunger to know Him. When we recognize our heart's cry for a relationship is also a need for God, we will no longer feel lack in our singleness. We will only experience the ache of emptiness if we don't go to the true source for our deepest need to be met.

I am a Dr. Pepper addict. I know. It's terrible. I love how healthier choices have seemed to become more popular these days. I realized I hadn't caught the recent trend, when I walked into a young adult conference carrying a large Dr. Pepper from McDonalds. My 32 ounce Styrofoam cup stood out against the sea of water bottles so obviously I threw it in the garbage can, after no less than a few moments in the lobby. This may sound drastic but it felt so very out of place. It, meaning me, because I clearly hadn't caught the health trend and was still completely reliant on the high fructose corn syrup and caffeine that would keep me alert and awake during the upcoming session. Needless to say, it was a struggle.

My body craves Dr. Pepper. It really does. The crisp, cold, sweet and refreshing taste is unmatched by any other soda. Of course, this is merely my opinion, but one I hold at high esteem. But even though my body craves Dr. Pepper it needs water. Your life may be craving a boyfriend, a best friend, a new job, a fresh start…but what it really needs is a deeper relationship with God.

I can tell when my body has had enough of sodas and sweets and all things full of carbs that I enjoy without much limitation. I can tell when what I need becomes what I crave and when I become thirsty for water, water becomes the most fulfilling choice. In those times, if I reach for a Dr. Pepper, it doesn't satisfy and normally even makes me feel worse.

In the same way, if we consistently reach out to find the satisfaction for that desire to be loved, wanted, cherished and known in friendships, relationships, etc., we'll keep coming up short and may even end up feeling worse. Needing God is like needing water. His presence satisfies like no other. His Word is true. His love sustains your very life. These remain true, no matter our season or circumstance. You may want Dr. Pepper but you need water. You may want to be dating but you need His presence. Soon what you need will become what you crave and emptiness will give way to being completely satisfied in Him.

Not only that, but God's love will meet your every need without any of the side effects of sugary carbonation. His love for you will never come up short or let you down. He remembers every detail. He pursues you in every moment. He sees you as beautiful and worthy of His affection. He'll never decide that another is more worthy of His love. His love is for you. No other person, hobby or relationship can do that.

If you nurture and cultivate your relationship with God it will become the foundation of all other things you will experience in this life. Friendships will come and go. You may date, you may not. Stability with school and careers and life may get rocky and feel uncertain. Plans may not fit in the time frame you had hoped. If your life's foundation is in relationship with God, when hard seasons come they won't be able to shake you.

Dr. Pepper is super fun and delicious and I have no plans of quitting any time soon, but it has its rightful place. I understand the balance between when it's what I want and when it's what I need. If I begin to feel that I *need* something that's not good for me, it is likely because I am deficient in what I truly need.

If I become deficient in my relationship with God I get hungry for love and affection and begin to meet that need in a way that won't really satisfy. It is easy for me to wall myself up behind independence and self-sustaining busyness because it keeps me from feeling the pain and seeming rejection of my singleness. Maybe for you it's an on-and-off-again relationship, or the constant revolving door of guys, food, or social media.

Where We Need it Most..

We need to be loved, valued, treasured and pursued. We need to know that we are beautiful. But we need it most from *Him*. Knowing God and walking in relationship with Him will answer every single one of these desires of your heart.

Jesus said that we would never be alone because He would send the Holy Spirit to be with us, in us (Romans 8:11), for us (John 16:13) and a direct connection between us and the Father (Ephesians 2:18). How amazing is that? So, really, the offer of the Holy Spirit is a declaration that He has forever abolished loneliness. In Him, we are never alone (John 14:16) and have everything we need.

Maybe today you feel alone. Maybe there are constant reminders in your life that point to the fact you spend a lot of time on your own. But you're not! God is right there with you offering all the love and companionship that you need. He cares about every exciting and mundane detail of your life, every high and every low.

I know this sounds like a simple solution, easier said than done, and one that you may not believe will truly satisfy the deeper longing in your heart. So how do we do this in a practical way?

Instead of being alone, be with Him. It is that simple. Just like the perspective of the donkey, you can either get buried in your loneliness or you can climb out of it. The fact that you are single may not change, at least not right away, but single does not equal lonely.

Be present in your relationship with God like you would hope to have in the companionship of that friend or relationship. Allow the depths of your soul to cry out for the one thing it really needs, a deeper relationship with God.

You don't have to strive for His attention or His love. You don't have to work for it or perform for it. Let go of the pressure you're under to be in that perfect relationship already and simply be with Him.

For me, life has color again. I still travel alone sometimes like I did when I first started out at just eight years old, but my pit has been filled with the hope that I am never alone, when I remain connected to the Author of my life and Lover of my soul, Jesus Christ.

Right here, in this moment, you also have the opportunity to begin climbing out of what may feel like a dark and lonely season. You have the ability to redefine your single season in terms of being perfectly loved, wanted, cherished and known. You don't have to wait for a new BFF or boyfriend or even to get married! Whether you're starting from the top of the hill or the bottom, there is more love for you than you are experiencing right now, and my greatest prayer is that you will find it in a deeper relationship with God.

"

YOU *love*
& desire
TO HAVE ME ♡
as your very own.

PSALM 6:4 TPT

Abba,

You know my name. More than that, You have redeemed me so I am Yours. When I'm in over my head, I know You're still with me. Even when storms rage, they can't overwhelm me. When I feel stuck between a rock and a hard place, I know that's not where it'll end because I am Yours. You paid a huge price for me. That's how much I mean to You. That's how much You love me! No matter the cost, You'll do whatever it takes just for me. And You've already paid it! (Isaiah 43:1-3)

Day after day You are with me (Matthew 28:20) so I can be strong and courageous. Rather than be afraid, I am encouraged because You are with me in every decision (Joshua 1:9). There's no need for me to fear or be anxious because You are my strength and my help, my stability and support (Isaiah 41:10).

You are right here with me. You won't let me down. I won't be intimidated or even give my fear a second thought because You won't ever leave me (Deuteronomy 31:6). Thank You for the Friend I have in the Holy Spirit! Because of You I am never alone and always have someone with me (John 14:16). Even when I face dark valleys, I won't be afraid, because You walk alongside me (Psalm 23:4).

You've always been here for me. Even when those that were supposed to take care of me walked out and left me, You took me in (Psalm 27:9-10).

I cannot escape Your Presence. You are wherever I am no matter where I go; You are there for me. Even in the dark, You see me and light my life (Psalm 139:7-12). Take me by the hand and lead me with your wisdom. You are all I want both now and forever. You are rock-firm and faithful. Once left out, You are now my home (Psalm 73:23-28).

I'm not letting go of You (Psalm 16:8),

Your Daughter

Chapter Two: A Single Perspective

How do you see it? If you're anything like me, you'd rather already be on the other side of single and into your next season. This is one of those things that you really have zero control over.

It is true that if you are really pursuing marriage for the right reason, there's not a whole lot you can do to change the process or speed it up. Disappointing, I know. If only it were something simple that we could change on our own. But matters of the heart can't be skipped or rushed because they are a needed part of our journey. Aren't we thankful God gives us what we need over what we just want? Sometimes we can ask for some crazy things that a loving Father just knows better than to give us.

Here's the deal. There are seasons when I have been perfectly content not being married. It's as if the desire was just a whisper in a very loud world of other ventures and aspirations, along with the fulfillment of other dreams. And then there were times when every picture on social media seemed to scream how alone I was. Friends ten years younger were having children and living the life that, quite frankly, made me feel left out. Can you relate? Every "in a relationship" post, dreamy date night photo, engagement announcement, wedding photo… they all made my emotions run crazy, as though my loneliness was at the expense of their happiness.

How We're Seeing It

Aren't we longing for the same joys they are experiencing? The difference between being genuinely happy for them and being completely wrecked is our perspective. It's not so much about what we're seeing, but how we're seeing it. Do you see their love or that you're not in a relationship? Do you see their joy or that you're alone? Our perspective is a fruit of the condition of our heart and directly related to our relationship with God.

I've spent many holidays, weeks, months and seasons being down-and-out because of what I was missing by being alone. But I was alone. Yes, I was single, but I was also alone because I had walls up that didn't let love in from anyone else because I felt jaded that I didn't have the one love I wanted most.

What if you are going to be single for another year, five years, ten years? Wouldn't you like that time to be spent savoring every experience from a place of contentment? They certainly can be spent being miserable because of a perspective rooted in what you're lacking. You may still go to prom without a boyfriend or back to an empty house after the New Year's party, but it doesn't have to feel like the bottom of the barrel. It doesn't have to feel bad at all. It's all in your perspective!

You may not be able to speed up the process, but you can do single right! Savoring single will reap benefits that far outweigh being sad and lonely or just plain miserable for however long this season lasts.

Adjusting our perspective about being single will help our hearts from becoming discouraged in the waiting. Love is a common preoccupation of our thoughts. Because of this it is important how we are looking at it. There are two sides to the same love coin. The pity party is easy but makes things much harder in the long run. Contentment is harder at first but reaps greater benefits in the future. Either way our perspective is up to us.

Coming up out of a rut is up to us and the perspective we choose. I lived a lot of years living in the low of waiting and it made life completely miserable. Am I still waiting? Yes. But now I am living from a much better place because of my new perspective. Life is too good, too rich and has too much to offer to live in the dredges over something I have little power to change.

Becoming content with being single doesn't mean you give up the hope for being married. It also doesn't always mean it's going to be easy. Waiting can be hard. But life is hard. Single people have it hard. Married people have it hard. Broken-up people have it hard. It's hard having kids, not having kids, sending kids away, kids never leaving. You get my drift? Being single has its difficulties and challenges and hard days, but so does every other season of life.

I get it. If you are somewhere between your dreams of a re
meeting that dreamy guy, you've got some time on your h
live your life in that in-between is what makes all the diffe

I encourage you to find ways to live life with that time instead of just
waiting the time away: waiting to enjoy life and pursue dreams, waiting on
the couch hoping to be called, waiting by the phone for a text, waiting for
a fairy tale ending to begin experiencing life. If you feel like life is passing
you by while you are waiting for your one-day guy, it probably is passing
you by. We can get so focused on one dream that waiting on it to come
to pass shuts everything else down by default. It's easy for this to happen
without even realizing it, where moments of seclusion seem to become
more common and feeling isolated becomes a recurring theme. If this is
you and you want to start living again in your waiting season, allow other
dreams to wake back up.

So Much More..

Your life is so much more than one dream coming true because time
never stops! It's faithful and constant and you spend it whether you want
to or not. You can't get more of it or get it back if you waste it. Your time is
precious! Your life is special! Stop waiting on a relationship or marriage to
live fully because this world needs you, and it won't get much of you waiting
on your couch for all your dreams to come true. You are not left out. You
are not alone. This moment counts. Today matters.

During this in-between time I know that sometimes you feel unnoticed.
I know that your heart feels unloved. I know your beauty seems invisible
sometimes and that your humor goes unappreciated. I know that sometimes
you'd give anything just to have someone sit next to you on the couch to
watch a movie, hold your hand as you walk down the hall, or to be thinking
about you on your worst day.

I know. It's a real longing and legitimate desire. God built those desires into
the fabric of our being so that we would, above all, long for this kind of love
with Him. Coming into this kind of love with God is not the replacement
of our dream for marriage, but can be the foundation of every other dream
He wants to fulfill in our hearts during every season of our lives.

you're always looking forward to something to find your happiness, you won't be happy in your now. Likewise, if you feel your greatest happiness is or could have been somewhere in your past, you have no hope for it in your future.

So, take courage. Hold on. He's with you in the waiting. He's not at the end of the aisle, making you walk alone... He's the one taking every step with you until you meet your forever-guy at the altar. He then turns with you both, hand in hand, and walks with you for the rest of your journey, as one.

How Others See It

While you're waiting, people who care about you will offer their words of encouragement. It won't likely ever help, but they love you and simply don't know what else to say. Maybe you've heard it sound something like this. "Girl, when you stop looking for him he'll find you." Or, "Once you are content with not having him is when God can trust you with him." Sprinkle in a little, "Maybe you're just too picky." And the salt on the open wound, "It's better to stay single than to settle!"

This has happened more times than I could count but one in particular stands out above the rest.

I have a 92-year old grandfather, whom I lovingly call Papaw. He's a tall man, thinly built and has worked hard his entire life. My Grandma, however, was quite a bit shorter and had a plumper figure. He liked her that way; he even picked her out because of it. She caught his eye during one of her daily trips to the store for ice cream, and it's been a life full of wonderful stories since. He joined the Air Force in its first year back in 1947, and they married before she ever finished high school.

He always tells me how proud he is of me. He loves that I have always been able to work hard, like him, and have an upstanding job. He is amazed at all the opportunities that have come my way and tells my stories like they are some of his very own. A strong work ethic has been a huge part of his life and I feel like he connects with me in this way. As for getting married, however, he has never encouraged me to date or get married. This he reminds me of often as well.

This time we were having a visit, as usual. My sister and I were sitting across from each other with him to my left. The topic of my singleness came up somehow and like he was back in the Air Force again, he dropped a bomb that I didn't expect nor had any way to prepare for. I don't think he meant to and probably never realized that he did, but he said it. He said something like, "Well no sense in trying to get married now since you're past your prime." My jaw dropped. Not in a "oh no, he didn't" kind of way, but in an "I can't believe my Papaw just said that" kind of way. It was a dropped jaw but a full smile at the same time. I looked at my sister square across the room and we laughed. It was rather hilarious. Papaw just told me I was past my prime in the same tone as he had just told me what he had eaten for lunch.

The earth didn't shatter. My heart didn't break. I certainly wasn't expecting it, but he didn't say anything I hadn't already heard. He's just probably the only one that's ever said it so matter-of-fact and with no apology on his perspective. He probably didn't even realize he said it. But he did. For a man who married so young, a woman in her thirties clearly qualifies for one who is past their prime.

Okay. Maybe you aren't in your thirties yet. Maybe you are younger and praying like I did, that by the time you turn thirty, you won't still be single. Maybe for you it isn't totally about being married yet, but to be in a significant relationship that might eventually lead to marriage. Either way, it isn't just about being thirty plus. You could be in your twenties and already feel like your best days are behind you and you've missed it. Your prime is anything beyond when you thought you would have been married. For some of us, that's a pretty young number. For others, we have already decided to live a little more, graduate college first, or maybe establish a career. Statistics show many more of us gals are waiting much longer to get married than before. But either way, if you are beyond when you thought you should have been married, you may already feel like you're past your prime.

When my Papaw said that, even though I know how much he loves me, my honest response was "I'm not." Culture may say that I am because I am older than their pre-determined age range for an ideal relationship. My Papaw, who grew up in a generation who married much younger, may think I am. Even I could be tempted to believe I am, if I compare myself to my two already-married sisters. But I'm not. And neither are you.

This moment allowed me to see the perspective I was looking through. My response wasn't rooted in culture, family expectations or even experience. My confident response was rooted in seeing my singleness better from God's perspective than I have in any season before.

When these opportunities to respond come, take a moment to reflect on how you are seeing things and from which perspective. Sometimes words will fly out of our mouth before we ever realize what we are saying. Weigh those words to recalibrate your heart back to seeing things God's ways.

How God Sees It..

When I think of someone in the Bible who was "past their prime" it would have to be Sarah. If you're familiar with her story, you probably just grumbled...ugh! Let's be real, I feel you on this one!

In case you're not familiar, Sarah was Abraham's wife. Abraham was called by God to leave his hometown and travel to a foreign land that would become the Promised Land. They had many adventures, ups and downs. One of Sarah's lowest was that she remained barren years after marriage. Barrenness was regarded as a curse in biblical times and she felt much shame from her inability to give Abraham an heir to continue his lineage. But God showed up, because He is faithful. He might not work according to our calendar but He is faithful still. Sarah got pregnant and gave Abraham a son, but not until she was 90!!! Yep, ninety. Nine. Zero. Ninety (Genesis 17:17)!

Many of us don't like this story because Sarah had to wait such a long time. We hesitate to identify with the long season of waiting, so thinking of her as someone past her prime is not the kind of example we really want to hear about; even though, this is a great example for us to see into the Father's heart and how He sees our singleness.

Let's pick up in her story before her promise happened. She laughed. Sarah laughed. She heard the messenger tell her husband that she was going to have a baby. With an anxious heart wondering if it could really happen, she laughed. Culture had told her that she had missed her chance. I'm sure some ladies made it hard for her as the years went on. I'm sure some pitied her and tried to make her feel better saying some of those similar things we hear so often. She had sided with the lie that her dream was too big and too far gone to happen to her. Her circumstances seemed unchangeable, and she doubted that what God said could be true.

But God didn't care that she was 90. Her Father in Heaven looked beyond society's opinions and culture's standards and reached out to His daughter, whose heart still longed for the destiny God had sown into her life before she was ever born. Sarah had to wait a long time to see her promise fulfilled. You likely won't have to wait quite as long, but waiting still, I want your heart to understand that God is faithful to you and keeps the promises He has made to you. The destiny He sowed into your being before He formed you in your mother's womb is still there. It may look different than what you've imagined, but it can't be diminished or tarnished. It won't lessen with time or age. It's sure and true. And it's yours to walk out to the extent that you trust and rely on Him.

God is faithful even when we don't have perfect trust. Sarah wasn't perfect. She faltered in her faith. She even tried to make it happen her own way and created a big mess in the process. If you feel like you've completely messed up your life, so much so that God can no longer move on your behalf or fulfill the dreams in your heart, you are simply not big enough to be able to do that. We may falter in our trust, but God remains faithful. We may waste a lot of time, money, emotion or energy going down the wrong road, but God always provides a way out. We may be walled in, boarded up, cold hearted and isolated, but God is the God of breakthroughs.

I know that being single for longer than you hoped seems like an unchangeable circumstance because our best efforts to be prettier, funnier, smarter and more available seem worthless against a status that hasn't changed. But. God. Single now or single forever God is good and the more our perspective aligns with His, the more we will live this life fully no matter our status.

We can learn from Sarah that society has had these age ranges that predict your ideal age to be single, married and have kids since way back when. God's plan was bigger then and is bigger for you now. So make now your prime. Don't passively wait for it to happen to you. Take initiative and make life now the best you've ever had. Do that and you'll always be living in your prime... not looking forward to it or thinking you've already spent it.

"So, take courage. Hold on. He's with you in the waiting. He's not at the end of the aisle, making you walk alone… He's the one taking every step with you until you meet your forever-guy at the altar. He then turns with you both, hand in hand, and walks with you for the rest of your journey, as one."

"

He is making
EVERYTHING
right in the end.

PSALM 7:17 TPT

Abba,

Though it is hard for me to understand, I know that You are not actually late in keeping Your promises (2 Peter 3:9). You aren't angry at me or holding a grudge against me. You aren't vengeful toward me or treating me like I deserve because of my sin. You are the fullness of mercy and grace and how rich is Your love towards me! The strength of Your love can't be measured with earthly scales. You are a loving Father toward me and know me completely (Psalm 103:8-14).

You are the source of life, my very home, and I join myself with You never to be separated (John 15:5-8). Here I am, right where You want me, with endless grace and mercy in Jesus. I trust in You for salvation, after all, it was Your idea from the beginning. I didn't make myself and I can't save myself, it's all such a wonderful gift. You created me to save me so I could join in on Your wondrous plan (Ephesians 2:7-10).

Thank You for considering me worthy to partner with You! You took a chance on me, trusting me with all You've given me. You've always been merciful because I've made a lot of mistakes along the way. But You smothered my faith with love and grace to anoint me and fill me. Jesus Christ came to save, and I am proof, otherwise, I never would have made it (1 Timothy 1:14-19). But now, I am bursting with how You've come through for me (Psalm 13:6)!

Daughter and friend (2 Corinthians 5:19),

Your Daughter

Chapter Three: Finding Purpose in Single

I subconsciously thought that my purpose in life was to be a good Christian, a good wife one day and then a good mother. This was ingrained in me through the influences that I allowed to speak into my life like media, family and music.

Let's take movies for instance. How many have you seen that were based on a romantic relationship? Could you count them? What was the first movie you saw about a guy and a girl? Could you remember that far back? Then there is family, how many times were you asked growing up if you liked any boys at school? Dating anyone? Been in any serious relationships? What about music? We sing songs karaoke-style driving around to the tune of love whether lost, pursued, broken or just beginning. This is only a small list of voices that can become a sea of reasons why we believe we should already be dating or married.

From these same voices, I was hearing and seeing all the ways life was supposed to play out. Getting married became the main dream I looked forward to. As a result, I felt like I was missing a big portion of who I was supposed to be because I wasn't married yet. Year after year of unchanging circumstances heaped shame on my heart causing me to believe I was a huge disappointment. Coupled with the desire to be wanted and to be loved, it led me into depression. Because I felt like my purpose was rooted in a circumstance I couldn't change; the course of my life felt hopeless.

I've now come to the realization that my purpose isn't to get married. I may get married one day, but that doesn't mean it is my purpose in life. Get this. If your purpose is based on anything less than knowing Christ and making Him known, than you've sold yourself short for a purpose defined by culture or circumstance, rather than by God.

When I found my purpose in knowing God, it began to make all the difference! Here's how it all started.

I took part in a 21-day fast at my church. This is a time we set aside every January to really press into God through concentrated times of prayer and worship. This year was different as God totally engaged my heart in a way that I had never felt Him, heard Him or seen Him before. It was breathtaking! It made me even more hungry, so I was at every prayer meeting I could attend.

One night during prayer God and I had a conversation. I love that He isn't just the God that splits the seas, overthrows kingdoms and walks on water. He's the God that cares about the issues of my heart and desires to help me like no one else can. He's that whisper to my heart that brings warmth in a way that I know it's Him speaking.

We were praying about dreams and I began to think of what the primary dream of my life had been. Of course, I knew it was to be married. In response, He lovingly took me through a process of showing me that I had given up every other major dream He had for me, in pursuit of that one dream. I broke. Like the ugly kind of crying, need a whole box of tissues broke. It hurt on the inside but I knew it was exactly what I needed. God is a BIG dreamer and I had put my entire life in the box of this one dream. This one purpose for my life had swallowed up all the other ones.

I still lived out other dreams but it was always with a conscious pursuit of being found by "him." For instance, I went to conferences often preoccupied by the thought "he may be here." I even bought clothes thinking, "I may meet him wearing this." I went out to eat with girl friends, but remained aware of who else may be there. I was always "on" and it was exhausting. I also felt like a constant failure. I felt like because my face got oily, or my makeup faded, or my outfit was not brand new, or my hair was too flat that I had missed my chance of being seen and then noticed and then picked.

In a way, my purpose was wrapped in the dream of a relationship no matter what I was doing or where I was going. It had become a burden but I hadn't realized it until this night in prayer.

Purpose Redefined

It was in that moment that God began to redefine my purpose, so much so that six months later I tattooed it on my arm. I am not saying you have to get a tattoo, but this was such an epic moment in my life. The health of my heart and the direction of my life shifted. I wasn't consumed by it anymore. It wasn't the first thought when I walked into the room or the last thought before I went to bed. I felt a freedom I didn't realize I needed and never wanted to go back to the old me. Living from purpose, my newfound purpose in Christ, made everything else make sense.

Our purpose is not to get married, to have kids, get a good education or establish a great career. Our purpose isn't to make a lot of money or to be a good Christian. Our purpose is to know God and to live out of that relationship.

> "Steep your life in God-reality, God-initiative, God-provisions. Don't worry about missing out. You'll find all your everyday human concerns will be met." Matthew 6:33 MSG

Being single does not mean you are living a lesser life, nor does being married mean life will be more fulfilled. Your life lived as single girl does not mean it is deficient or lacking. Let me level with you. Your life is as full or as empty as you want it to be. If you reduce your happiness and life fulfillment to the fulfillment of one dream, you will be empty and unfilled until that dream comes to pass.

Though marriage is a beautiful experience of this life, it's not at the core of our purpose. Your purpose is not marriage; therefore, you are not lacking because you are not married. Your purpose is not to be a mom; therefore, you are not lacking if you have not given birth to children. Your purpose is to know God and to live out of that relationship with Christ.

> "This is eternal life, that they may know You, the only true God, and Jesus Christ whom You have sent." John 17:3 NASB

If this is our purpose than we must understand why God sent Jesus in the first place. Yes, God created the world and that world sinned. Because of that sin Jesus had to die on the cross. At my core I believed that Jesus had to die because I was a sinner that couldn't pay to clear my slate so I could get into Heaven when this life was over. True. But that was only part of it.

Before the foundations of the world God knew that we were going to sin. So before He created the first ray of light or drop of water, before he breathed into the dust for Adam to live, before all of creation, He had a plan to redeem us from being separated from Him.

> "For you know that God paid a ransom to save you from the empty life you inherited from your ancestors. And it was not paid with mere gold or silver, which lose their value. It was the precious blood of Christ, the sinless, spotless Lamb of God. God chose him as your ransom long before the world began, but now in these last days he has been revealed for your sake." 1 Peter 1:18-20 NLT

That's what sin does, it separates (Romans 5:12). It's as easy as a child walking along a path in the park and catching a glimpse of a big balloon. Without realizing it you've let go of your daddy's hand to follow it down the way. At the realization that you are no longer with him, his heart drops to the bottom of his chest and with angst he frantically searches for you. You aren't looking for him though, because you don't realize yet that you are lost. You are simply fixated on how the sun glows off that shiny balloon.

Though you are separated, you may not realize all the danger that surrounds. The thief that wants your coin purse. The kidnapper that wants a ransom for returning you. The perverted man that wants to harm you. You don't see all of this. You simply see a shiny balloon. Your dad has all of these dangers and more running through his mind because he knows. He knows what trouble lies waiting for you when you are apart from him. With his best effort, he pursues you. He calls out your name but you can't hear him. The crowd is noisy and that balloon has your focus. Sin separates us and allows harm to find us in a way that it never could, if we were still holding our daddy's hand.

Yes, Jesus came to remove sin, and his blood was the only thing that could. But he removed the stain of sin so we could come close, hold his hand, and walk through life in relationship with him. He doesn't just want you clean, He wants you close. This is the purpose of the Cross. This is the purpose for our lives, to live holding on to Him. Just like a daughter trusts her dad's hands to lead her and catch her if she falls, she also enjoys being close and enjoying the walk together.

Singleness. Dating. Marriage. Kids. Careers. Hobbies. Memories. Dreams. Each flow out of that one purpose to know God! Being single and not knowing Christ is empty. Being married and not knowing Christ is empty. Having kids without knowing God is still empty. Careers and hobbies without a relationship with God is still empty. Your life is as full or as empty as you choose it to be.

Our lives are composed of spirit, soul and body. We are spirit first because our Father God is spirit and we were created like Him and in His image (Genesis 1:26). We have a soul from which our desires and affections are directed by our mind, will and emotions. These two dwell in our physical bodies. Your true self is your spirit but is most often the least regarded.

> Spirit, Soul & Body
> "Now may the God of peace make you holy in every way, and may your whole spirit and soul and body be kept blameless until our Lord Jesus Christ comes again." 1 Thessalonians 5:23 NLT

> Spirit & Soul
> "For the word of God is alive and powerful. It is sharper than the sharpest two-edged sword, cutting between soul and spirit, between joint and marrow. It exposes our innermost thoughts and desires." Hebrews 4:12 NLT

Spirit
"No one can know a person's thoughts except that person's own spirit, and no one can know God's thoughts except God's own Spirit." 1 Corinthians 2:9-11 NLT

There's an old story about two dogs that fight. One dog was thin and frail, the other was strong and robust. Upon being asked which one wins, the owner responds, "the one I feed."

Our spirit, soul and body all cry out for something. Our bodies need food, water, rest, etc. Our souls seek pleasure and comfort. Our spirit cries out for the nearness of Abba Father.

"For you have not received a spirit of slavery leading to fear again, but you have received a spirit of adoption as sons by which we cry out, "Abba! Father!"" Romans 8:15 NASB

But which one do you most often feed? Our bodies and souls may seem to bark the loudest, but it's only in feeding our spirit that our soul and body also find proper nourishment. If we leave out the spiritual part of our being, we leave out the foundation of our existence and cannot function properly in the other two.

This explains why the root cause of our feeling of abundance or deficiency in life is not a relationship with a man, it's a relationship with God. Because feeding any part of our soul or body will only pacify the deepest need in our life which is a spiritual need, our need for Abba Father.

Is your purpose rooted in a relationship with Christ or in a circumstance like getting married or being in a relationship?

My prayer is that, like me, you will step into a totally different world of fullness, assurance, hope, faith, strength and courage. Being single doesn't have to be a season you struggle through, praying it ends quickly. It can be a beautiful part of your life. True happiness is found in contentment that's rooted in a relationship with Christ. From that place, your deepest needs are met in Him.

So While Single, Savor It! ....

In the next few chapters, we'll walk through some of the following ways you can begin to savor being single. In my journey, I have experienced where challenge turned to strength, depression turned to joy, hopelessness turned to faith, and loss turned to redemption. I pray the same for you! Here's some of what we'll be talking about:

- Loving and being loved doesn't have to wait until your one-day guy shows up.
- The what, how's and why's of Purity.
- Adventure can still be a dream come true, whether you share it with someone or not.
- Developing a skillset will expand the horizons of your life.
- Discipleship helps build yourself while building someone else; the impact is infinite.
- Gifts are plentiful and meant to be opened and fully enjoyed.
- Finances spent well is an investment with an eternal value.
- Relationship rather than religion.
- Your life is now. Begin to savor it!

Sometimes we can get so caught up in what we've heard that we stop hearing. I encourage you to open your heart to hear and listen to a different perspective about being single. It's okay to let that wall down and open your heart to hear again. Take it all in. Pray about it. Read and search the Scriptures. And then allow the Holy Spirit to bring adjustments, wherever they may be needed, to encourage and redirect your life into the abundantly above He created you for.

Single will be beautiful again and love doesn't have to wait until the "Happily Ever After".

"

i take hold of
your **PRAYERS**
TO ANSWER
them ➤➤➤ ••• ➤ *all.*

PSALM 6:9 TPT

Abba,

When I cry out for help, I know You hear me and are ready to rescue me (Psalm 34:17). And because through Jesus I have open access to You, I come before You to simply ask for what You are already ready to give me. I need Your mercy and I receive it (Hebrews 4:14-16). Because of Your Word, I can be sure that You are listening when I come into Your presence. Knowing that You are listening gives me confidence that I already have what I have asked for according to Your will (1 John 5:14).

I've left the comfort of evil so now I call out to You and it is music to Your ears. As soon as You hear me, You answer. You don't ignore my cry but stick with me because Your love is loyal (Psalm 66:17-20). You don't answer the wishes and wants of sinners, but as Your child, You hear every detail of my voice (John 9:31).

You see me when I keep my mouth from evil and hurtful words, cultivating good and pursuing peace. Your proud approval eagerly seeks to hear and answer my heart's desire (1 Peter 3:10-12). Because I know you listen with every fiber of your being, I will never stop praying…

I love You because You hear me and know my voice (Psalm 116:1-2),

Your Daughter

Chapter Four: Finding Love in Single

I was always tall for my age. One of my teachers in high school even called me "Too Tall." I grew up with makeover and model shows and had dreams of becoming a model one day. I think somewhere in our hearts we may all have had this dream at one point, like being the most beautiful girl in the room, or being the desire of guys and the envy of girls, or even finally sticking it to the ones that made fun of us and proving to ourselves that we were worth more than the labels they had placed on us.

My favorite part of those shows were the before-and-afters. I dreamed of having the chance of being made over and becoming the best version of myself at the hands of professionals who saw the potential in me. I practiced my runway walk like the girls on model shows. I even bought my first pair of stilettos at twelve years old and practiced walking in the house until I had them mastered.

I felt like becoming a model would mean I was beautiful. I didn't see it when I looked in the mirror and others didn't either in the way I was treated. But if I had the chance at a makeover, there was hope. At least that's how I felt.

I think sometimes we can see our pursuit of a relationship like a makeover that makes us something more than we are now. We dream that we will feel more loved, wanted, cherished and known in the same way that my becoming a model would make me feel beautiful. We hope it will finally be the way to feel loved that we don't often experience being single.

In this makeover pursuit of love, are we pursuing the impact being in a relationship would have on us more than love itself?

Most of what we have come to know love to be is an elevated sense of who we become once in a romantic relationship. We see the before-and-after and want to look like the after. We want the Pinterest wedding and the Instagram marriage.

I believe love is so much more than how it makes us feel. Because if we base love on how it makes us feel, then when we lose those feelings and love will seem lost. So, if love isn't these feelings we've come so accustomed to believing, then what is love? I'm so glad you asked because I wanted to know the same thing too.

What Is Love?

I think the only viable place to find what love really is all about is in the greatest love letter ever written. A star-crossed lovers kind of love that goes beyond eternity is also intimately known in the deepest places of our hearts. Who is our Romeo? None other than God himself.

He's the only one that qualifies to define love because He is love. It's not that He simply loves us in the way that we love each other or that Romeo loved Juliet. To love is a verb. His Love is an unchanging attribute of His very nature. Love is who He is. It is the essence of His being. If we are to know what love is we must look to Love Himself. He is the ultimate prototype, the supreme example, the express image of the very love we desire!

There are over 200 accounts of the word "love/loved" in the New Testament alone. 200 plus times God used the word love to tell us something about His heart and ours.

65 times He communicated His love toward us.
60 times He talked about our Love for Others.
43 times Love was used as a noun.
29 times He described our Love for God.
20 times He referenced Love for other things.

I've included my listing of Scriptures in the "Love Study" at the back of the book, so you can read through and soak on the topic from the Word itself.

Two huge things popped out to me during this word study on love:

First, God loves us!

Second, we are to love others! Whoa! The same words again, and again, and again. He's really driving the point home here. And out of those 60 verses about loving other people, a mere six are specifically about a marriage relationship.

What I gather from this is that our pursuit of love in a romantic relationship is largely disproportionate to the way God intended us to experience love in our lives. When we limit love to romance we truly minimize the potential of how much love our lives could hold.

But romantic love is primarily how we see love expressed and has become the cultural norm of our society. Even healthy families aren't represented well enough in entertainment to bolster a high expectation of love between parents and their children or even between spouses. This begins at a very young age. Think about how many Disney films lack either or both parents. But equally, how much these movies are centered around finding love, being loved and developing significant relationships. It's a perception ingrained in us before we knew differently.

But contrary to cultural perception, to pursue love is to pursue love itself, not romance or affection. Love according to the Word of God begins first in relationship with God. Then it flows through us and into others.

Understanding this released the pressure I was under to be in that perfect relationship already. In the same way that it would remove my need for a makeover to feel beautiful. It separates the before from the after and says that my now is okay. That being single is okay because now I don't have to wait on that relationship to experience love. I don't have to live loveless because I am single. I can know love, pursue love and be loved without having to wait for the circumstances of my singleness to change. And you can too.

To Know Love..

There is an illustration my children's church pastor used that I'll never forget. She asked the class, "Do you know about Abraham Lincoln?" We replied something like, "yeah, sure we do." Then she asked, "But do you *know* Abraham Lincoln?" We replied, "of course not, he lived a long time ago!" I can easily know about someone without ever knowing them. Our culture is filled with these types of relationships.

I ran into an old friend at the mall one day and remember saying, "Girl, it's so good to see you! I've kept up with you on Facebook. How's your son doing?" I knew about some things that had happened over the course of the last few years, but hadn't experienced any of them with her.

Actually knowing someone requires a connection, an exchange of who I am with who you are. This is what God desires in His relationship with you. To know love is to know God. He is love. The more you know Him, the better you understand love and absorb it into your very being. Knowing someone goes far beyond posts, pictures, facts and understanding. Knowing becomes an experience.

If you're asking, "Well then, how do I know God?" think about how you would get to know anyone else. Thinking back on one of my most recent new friendships that has developed into a close friendship, it began with communication. We'd talk at church and special events. Then she joined a ministry team I was already on and, working together, we got to know each other more. After that, we began to hang out for coffee or at her house. Eventually it turned into fun road trips and hours of great conversation.

Communication..

God has given us some great ways to communicate with Him. His Word and Prayer are a great place to start. By reading the Bible we get to hear what He has already said. He reveals so much about who He is, who you are, what He thinks about you. Not only that, we can pray scripture as a guide for what and how to pray.

> "All Scripture is inspired by God and is useful to teach us what is true and to make us realize what is wrong in our lives. It corrects us when we are wrong and teaches us to do what is right." 2 Timothy 3:16 NLT

"For the word of God is alive and powerful. It is sharper than the sharpest two-edged sword, cutting between soul and spirit, between joint and marrow. It exposes our innermost thoughts and desires." Hebrews 4:12 NLT

Then there is prayer. I feel like the church has made prayer so "super-spiritual" at times that we've lost the revelation of it at the expense of form and ritual. Prayer is an open channel of two-way communication. He speaks and I listen. I speak and He listens. There are so many studies on prayer that can help you develop a life of prayer, but at the root of it should always be the first two words that Jesus prayed when He modeled prayer for His disciples, "Our Father" (Matthew 6:9-13). Relationship. Knowing. An exchange between me and God because I know Him and He knows me.

"Rejoice in our confident hope. Be patient in trouble, and keep on praying." Romans 12:12 NLT

"Don't worry about anything; instead, pray about everything. Tell God what you need, and thank him for all he has done." Philippians 4:6 NLT

Partnership

When we open our lives to intentionally bring God into the decisions we make, consult His Word for direction and rely on His process, we increase our capacity to trust Him and our ability to hear from Him more clearly.

Trust in the Lord with all your heart; do not depend on your own understanding. Seek his will in all you do, and he will show you which path to take." Proverbs 3:5-6 NLT

Quality Time

You can spend time without quality but you cannot spend quality without time. Quality speaks of uninterrupted and undivided attention. Phone down. TV off. Door closed. Face to face. Time is the evidence of what is most important to you.

Knowing love in this season is not only possible, but it is within reach. Get alone with God and get to know each other. It's an investment of your time that reaps rewards in every other area of your life. This is a place of vulnerability and honesty; a safe place because He is Love and this is how He is towards you.

> "Love is large and incredibly patient. Love is gentle and consistently kind to all. It refuses to be jealous when blessing comes to someone else. Love does not brag about one's achievements nor inflate its own importance. Love does not traffic in shame and disrespect, nor selfishly seek its own honor. Love is not easily irritated or quick to take offense. Love joyfully celebrates honesty and finds no delight in what is wrong. Love is a safe place of shelter, for it never stops believing the best for others. Love never takes failure as defeat, for it never gives up." 1 Corinthians 13:4-7 TPT

You can always run to the one who has never stopped believing the best for you and find an open embrace into authentic relationship.

To Love ....

Love is not one sided. In natural relationships, we would call that unrequited love and it is torture. I know. I always seemed to fall for the guy that had zero interest in me. And then the guys I had zero interest in would fall for me. It's awkward and uncomfortable and leaves half of the equation hurt and broken and rejected. If you don't want to live that way, pursue the fullness of a two-sided relationship with the Lover of your soul that cares more for you than you could ever imagine.

God continually pours out the essence of who He is in love towards us without any guarantee that we will ever love Him in return. Some of His love will remain unrequited for all of eternity, but He pours it out anyway, because that's just how much He loves us. I wonder how anyone could ever reject such an invitation, at the same time knowing that I have at times. I have been unresponsive to His love. Cold. Indifferent. Apathetic. It sounds ridiculous, but when you feel rejected by imperfect love, perfect love seems unreal and impractical. How can God (Perfect Love) love me in my weakness, my mess, my struggles, my fears?

When I felt unlovable, unworthy of His sacrifice, ashamed of my choices, oppressed under heaviness, my heart grew cold and hard. Layer upon layer waxed over my soul sealing off, once again, the ache of loneliness and the grief of rejection.

> "And I will give you a new heart, and I will put a new spirit in you. I will take out your stony, stubborn heart and give you a tender, responsive heart." Ezekiel 36:26 NLT

What is the opposite to a stony and stubborn heart? A tender and responsive heart. When we begin to receive God's love by knowing Him, our response becomes the way that we love Him in return.

Sometimes there are thoughts that enter our minds when we hear about His love for us; thoughts like shame, guilt or condemnation, apathy and discomfort. These can serve as indicators that our heart needs His love more than we realize. When we begin to feel these things, there can also be a temptation to wax cold and shut love down so that you don't have to face them. But receiving God's love and loving Him in return is the only way to remove them from the equation completely.

So loving God is responding to Him. He doesn't need anything from you. He is much like that parent that doesn't need anything, making it super difficult to buy a present. It is so much easier to meet a need, but when there is no need to meet, the gift becomes solely an expression of love. Express your love to Him in a way that engages your whole heart. Give your best. Lay down the things that separate you from Him. Take time. Talk to Him. Sing, paint, dance, build, just be you to Him. Acknowledge Him and invite Him along. Like the mom that says "Don't buy me anything. All I want is for you to spend time with me, your hugs and your kisses." Your affection is His desire.

> "I love all who love me. Those who search will surely find me." Proverbs 8:17 NLT

Being loved while single is probably one of the hardest struggles we face. As humans we need to know that we are loved. To feel loved we love others but with expected reciprocation. If I love you, you will love me. If I help you, you will help me. This kind of love is not a gift but a loan. It comes with the hope that because I have loved I will be loved in return. A common pitfall to the love on loan program is that when you loan out your love it is depleted until it is returned. This is where the cycle of depression, loneliness and heartache repeats in our lives.

We know the guy that says, "If you love me you will..." is a love that comes with strings attached. If you don't do whatever he's wanting, he'll cut the strings and walk away. This isn't real love. We love to hate these kinds of guys in movies. But we can do this very thing in much more subtle ways. We can love only to be loved in return because we have a deficit in our love account that aches until there's a deposit, no matter how that deposit comes.

That's how girls fall into traps with guys like that. They become so depleted of love they'll compromise for just a taste of acceptance and affection to put even the smallest deposit back in their account. But you can't get full with love on loan so the cycle repeats itself, loneliness becomes chronic and the temptation to fill a right need the wrong way becomes harder to fight.

When you fill your life with God's love by knowing and responding to Him in relationship, He is the one that fills your love account. Then when you love others it's not out of need for love in return, but as a gift to enhance their lives.

You wouldn't think that to be loved would mean giving love away any more than a debit transaction would add money to your bank account. But it does. The more you open yourself to love God, His love floods in and fills you up but it doesn't stop there.

Sixty-plus times God tells us through the Scripture that we should love our neighbor and love one another and even our enemies. When we become a conduit of love from God to others, we experience love in the process, much like a water hose gets wet watering the grass and won't become dry as long as water is running through it.

It's a sacrifice to truly love others, to be there for them when you get nothing in return, to pour into someone else's life who may never pour back into yours, to regard those who have become forgotten by many, to love those who don't love themselves, to love those who are seemingly unlovable. But in this is the greatest of all and the very example we have in Christ Jesus. While we were engulfed in the stink and filth of our sin, He died for us without a guarantee that we would ever love Him in return, but that we would have the choice should we choose it. Wow!

> "There is no greater love than to lay down one's life for one's friends." John 15:13 NLT

Don't stop at just getting full of God's love but allow His love to flow through your life to someone else. Who around you could use some love? There are a million ways to show love and everyone is a candidate because everyone is a son or daughter of God!

Pursue love in its truest form – not to receive something in return, but to love for the sake of love. "Those who refresh others will themselves be refreshed." Proverbs 11:25 NLT. Those who love others will themselves be loved.

So, God loves us and we were made to love others. He pours in. We pour out. Your life being full of love is not contingent upon being in a relationship or getting married, because his love can never fill you like God's love can.

"

you empower me for
VICTORY
with your wrap-around
presence.

PSALM 18:35A TPT

Abba,

Because You are on my side, how can I not win? You already risked absolutely everything by sending Jesus, so there's nothing You would withhold from me (Romans 8:31). No detail passes Your notice, so I have no reason to be anxious or get upset. You've got me and You are with me for the long haul (1 Chronicles 28:20). On top of that, You didn't leave me or abandon me, but left me complete and with perfect peace by sending the Holy Spirit. I will not let things upset me to the point I feel there is no hope, because You will help me understand (John 14:27). Having You, I am fearless. I have no reason to be afraid of anyone or anything (Psalm 27:1).

You picked me. You haven't let me down. You're with me, so fear has no place. Strengthen me and help me, steady my feet as I lean into You (Isaiah 41:9-10). I can trust You from the depths of my being, so I won't try to make sense of everything, doing things my own way. I am listening for what You have to say for what I do and where I go, knowing that You'll keep me from wandering aimlessly or into harm's way.

Thank You for the promise that as I run to You and away from evil, my bones will be strong and my body full of health. I honor You with my everything, giving You my first and my best (Proverbs 3:5-9).

You have not called me to worry or believe the worst, but filled me with immense expectation eagerly seeking You for what's to come. Because I know You, I now know who I am. You are my Father. I am Your daughter. When I get what's coming to me, I know it's Your marvelous inheritance (Romans 8:15-17)!

Securely Yours,

Your Daughter

Chapter Five: Love, Practically

We have learned how to be quite efficient with our time as multi-tasking has gone to a whole new level. Quality time has suffered because our attention is constantly distracted between work, bills, obligations, social media, sports, etc., rather than just being present.

We have to be intentional not to carry this culture into our devotional time with God. I can read a couple of chapters of the Bible pretty quickly and get absolutely nothing out of it. I can check it off my reading plan and feel like I've been a good Christian for the day, without the Word exposing my heart and correcting my character. I can attend a 90-minute service on Sunday morning and feel like I've fulfilled my religious obligation to remain a part of the "holy club" without ever maturing my personal walk with God at home. I can do without ever becoming. The goal is to become the Word you read, become like the God you worship, become like the Christ you follow. This will only happen if you read, worship and follow with your heart engaged in relationship not duty.

So, s l o w d o w n ! Slow way down! Stop rushing it like you've added it to your life instead of it being your life. God isn't an accessory we add to make us feel better, He is the core foundation to everything. If our life is not rooted in Him it will falter most assuredly. You can't rush the foundation. You can't skip past the curing and maturing time. You can't add it after all the other things you prefer more. He's got to be first and He's got to have some time.

What Comes First?

How engaged are you in your relationship with God? You can know this by how you make your choices, how you spend your time, use your money and who you listen to when you have a decision to make. If He is simply an add-on, your heart won't be engaged and cannot receive the fullness of what He has for you.

Sometimes we treat our relationship with God and obedience to His Word much like our accessories. We'll take Him into consideration if it benefits us at the time, but if not we'll choose a different opinion that does. True Christianity isn't a cross you wear around your neck or even tattoo on your ankle; it's a permanent shift in your heart to become like Him in every way. This means we choose how He would choose, even if it costs us.

When you truly give your life to Christ it should look different than it did before. If you are still doing the same things, going the same places, talking the same way, thinking like you used to, now just bringing Jesus along and inserting Him into your same old life, you may have a form of religion that is lacking the true relationship He desires to have with you. We easily shape our lives after so many things. We are readily willing to shift preferences for a guy or best friend, but what about for God? If He's just an option when it suits, you don't have Him at all.

Seek first and engage your heart. When you read the Word, dig into it. Study it. Put yourself into the Scripture and visualize it. Don't just take it at face value. Since the Word is alive (Hebrews 4:12) you have the opportunity to receive fresh revelation every time you read it. Every time you press into hear God's heart through His Word. Then ask the Holy Spirit to reveal it to you (John 16:13). There is nothing like partnering with God to know God and become like Him! But it is invitation only and you hold the envelope in your hand. Invite him into your devotional time and engage your heart.

Quantity or Quality?

It's not how much you read, but allowing the Word to read you. It's not how many times you go to church, but how deep you allow the message to penetrate your heart.

I am athletically challenged. I was the girl in seventh-grade basketball that shot the ball into the other team's basket, scoring them a point and forever sealing my fate as tall but unathletic. This continued into my twenties when I joined an internship that had a heavy emphasis on fitness and health.

We ran laps, did hundreds of jumping jacks, without a break. I would be perfectly content if I never did another P90X video. Ever.

On the occasion that I hit the gym, my brain remembers that I was once active but quickly forgets how long ago that was, and so I attempt to do what I was once able to do. For instance, run a mile, not walk or jog, but run full out, in an effort to catch up on all that time I haven't been running. It never ends well. I leave feeling far more defeated than if I had just run at my capable level.

I have attempted this same strategy in my Bible reading. If I missed for a month, I'd try and read a month's worth in a day with good intentions of suddenly being a super Christian. Ending in failure and feeling defeated, I'd go another month without reading.

While taking on challenges to grow in your reading is good, if speed reading through the New Testament in 30 days means quantity rather than quality, then slow it down until you can read that much and still glean what the Word says to you. It's definitely not an overnight thing and you can't force yourself into a level you haven't lived through the process to achieve.

There are many tools to help us grow in our reading, in order to let the reading impact our lives. Things like W.O.R.D. (Write. Observe. Relate. Declare.), P.O.W.E.R. (Pray. Observe. Write. Envision. Respond.), S.O.A.P. (Scripture. Observation. Application. Prayer.), word mapping, color coding, outlining and so much more! Find one that works for you and go for it! There's no right or wrong. Just keep at it! I love how many of these either begin or end with prayer. Open a conversation with God into your reading and your relationship with Him will grow along with your understanding of His Word!

Everywhere. Every moment. Every situation. Every thought. He is bending down to hear you as you speak to Him, so open your heart and speak; then remain open to Him long enough to listen. When you hear, obey no matter the cost.

I love shopping in stores where the associates are engaged in my shopping experience. I spent a lot of years as a retail store manager, so I appreciate what good customer service looks like. To this day, I prefer to make purchases in stores with this personal touch of service. And when they do, I go out of my way to acknowledge those that do a great job! Some encouragement goes a long way.

I went into this store at a new mall in our area before Easter. I hadn't been clothes shopping in a long time because I hadn't felt like it. I wore my work uniform 50 to 60 hours a week, and when I was off, I just wanted to be comfy. Sunday mornings were the only time I really put any effort into fashion. I know, sad. But I went from store to store and found nothing. I mean nothing. I was so bummed that it was difficult. I wasn't even being picky. I just couldn't find anything!

While I was shopping, I was talking to God and said something like this, "God, why is this not fun for me? I used to love to shop but I am really not enjoying this." He responded in my heart and said, "Because it's not filling a need anymore." Boom! I felt the love of God just flow over me as I realized He had healed an area of my heart, and I didn't even realize it until that moment. I used to be depressed a lot and reverted to retail therapy as a solution. I racked up a whole lot of "stupid debt" (meaning money on a credit card that wasn't an investment into anything that really mattered) and wasted a lot of time and money in making myself feel better in a way that never worked. Shopping would be a reprieve and I could get my mind off my loneliness and sadness for a while.

That's not who I was anymore and in that moment, when God spoke inside my heart, I felt beautiful and light and free. Still hadn't found anything for Easter, but was content knowing God was with me and how much He had healed my heart.

I then walked into this one store and finally found a few things to try on. The girl that assisted me was helpful and brought together an entire outfit based on one skirt I picked up out of desperation. I don't even wear skirts! She made that experience special and stuck with me all the way through check out. It wasn't a commission store and I knew it. I made sure to complement her to the manager and kept the receipt so I could call it in to corporate.

She was sincerely engaged in my shopping experience and it made all the difference. One way she did this was by asking me open ended questions. Not just "How are you doing today?" which would return a one-worded and generic response like "Good," but "What can I help you find today?" That allowed me to express my frustration in not finding anything for Easter. By asking this way she demonstrated that she was interested in helping me, not just acknowledging my presence in her store.

Most of our prayers are framed like the first example. We talk to God and give him our list of wants and needs like it's a one-sided conversation, not really expecting Him to respond. Then go about our day as if the conversation was necessary but unimpactful. We, in a sense, acknowledge that God is "in our store" and we're there if He wants us, but then walk away without establishing trust. This breeds a shallow sense of relationship that feels generic and vague and isn't strong enough to count on when life becomes more than we can handle on our own.

Much like a sales associate that greets you but never offers genuine help, we know the difference between being present and being available. I'm not going to come out of the dressing room and ask for advice from a girl who didn't acknowledge that I was there. I don't trust that she cares enough.

When we approach God this way, most of us then turn to other things to fill a void we thought God should have filled. But did we ever really give Him a chance? Retail therapy, wrong relationships, abusive addictions, reoccurring habits and the like become our reprieve. We turn to these kinds of things when we don't have the assurance that God is really with us, and we are disappointed by the lack of depth in the experience we have with Him.

Instead, genuinely engage His presence and ask open ended questions. Deepen what you have with Him by talking to Him about anything and everything. Leave enough quiet space for Him to respond. I love the picture that David paints in Psalms when he says that God bends down to listen to us when we pray (Psalm 116:2). Oh, how intrigued He is with you and how He longs for you to hear what He is speaking to you personally. We can hear Him in many ways, but we have to be listening. We hear His heart primarily through His Word, as His Word is who He is (John 1). We also hear Him through a soft-spoken voice in our hearts or our conscience.

Don't allow God's love for you to be unrequited. Return the love that He has for you back to Him in a personal and engaging relationship where you speak to Him and allow Him to speak to you. This is how you become intimate and build a relationship of trust and meaning like we talked about before.

What About My Walls?

Think about what may be separating you from engaging fully into your relationship with God. Most of us know what that area is, whether we would like to admit it or not. We hold that area dear. It's something we're just not ready to let go. But holding on to that area is the very thing that is keeping us from our next level of knowing God and being known by Him.

Maybe it's unforgiveness towards someone who did something wrong against you. Maybe it's a "pet sin" that you feel isn't so bad on the scale of bad to worse and have justified in your heart that it's okay. Maybe it's shame that has caused you to hide because of what you've been through. Maybe it's a job, a boyfriend, an unhealthy friendship, an attitude, a habit, a vice, a lie about your identity. It could be a hundred different things.

Think about it for a minute. What takes place over my devotional time? How do I allow myself to be distracted instead of engaging my heart when I do read and pray and worship? What keeps me from going to church? That thing that's lingering in your mind that you're trying not to focus on. That's it! That is a wall between you and a free relationship with God.

Maybe it's not wrong per se, but what is wrong for you is wrong. James 4:17 NLT says "Remember, it is sin to know what you ought to do and then not do it." So maybe watching TV isn't a sin, but if TV is what is separating you from an engaging relationship with God then TV is sin for you. Same is true with magazines, social media, wrong friendships, unhealthy relationships, music, movies, books, jobs, etc. If the Holy Spirit is tugging on your heart to lay that thing down, it's for your good that you do.

Will it hurt? Yes. Will it be uncomfortable? Most likely. But will it be worth it? Absolutely!

Breaking down barriers starts with recognizing what those barriers are. Then you have to take steps to weaken their foundation in your choices so that they can begin to crumble in your life. Choices!

Find Scriptures in your Bible reading time to support what you want to see and meditate on them. Post them up in your room, on your mirror, in your car and remind yourself of your GOAL in Jesus. When old desires begin to draw you, think on these things and remind yourself of the benefit of saying "NO!"

So far in my relationship with God, I have laid down many things out of obedience to His tug on my heart. A few that stand out are secular music and TV/movies. I laid down secular music upwards of ten plus years ago. And it actually took doing it twice before I was completely finished with it. It wasn't until years after that when I looked back at seasons of my life, I could tell how the music that I listened to had dictated my emotions, desires, even my dreams and frustrations. It's not like I was listening to vulgar music or lyrics cluttered with foul language, but the moods and spirit behind the music certainly had a hand in directing my emotional clarity. That's a lot of power from something we engage with every day, probably without a second thought.

Years later He began to speak to me about TV and movies. This time was different, though, because I knew there was a struggle. I just wasn't ready to let go. TV and movies had become a vice, in a way, in that when I had them on, even in the background, I felt less alone. My time off was easily dictated by finding a new series to watch or renting or buying movies. I maintained some moral standards on what I would watch and over time it became difficult to find new things. So then more time was wasted trying to find something new. It became a dependency and it wasn't good.

I was convicted during altar calls at church as it would come to my mind during prayer. I knew, but I just couldn't. After some time of not relenting, God began to put the word "consecrated" on my heart. He brought it up consistently for a solid year before I caved. I know it's something that seems so simple, and maybe this isn't your thing, but God knew that in order to get me to a better place with Him, I'd have to let it go. And I did.

Just like when I finally laid down secular music, I saw the impact on my life rather quickly. I found a new love of reading and writing. I have more time to spend on other things. I read my Bible nearly every day and spend a lot more time in prayer and worship. These were not consistent patterns in my life while TV/movies had my attention. My emotions are not up-and-down as much. Images don't just pop in my head anymore. I am more alive to the presence of God because I am not numb in my senses with all the worlds imagery, messages and influence.

Those are mine. What are yours? Maybe it's not TV, movies or music. Maybe it is. But whatever it is that God is tugging on your heart to lay down, please do. Take it from me, a girl that's right there in it with you, that it's worth it. The reward is so much greater than the sacrifice.

He's just trying to get as much of His love to us as He can, but we have to help Him along the way, by partnering with Him and what He's asking us to do.

Where Do I Start?

I hope by now that you realize there's so much more love to experience and to share being single! You don't have to wait anymore! But if you have been waiting to be loved to love, then you're going to have to start somewhere to rejuvenate the cycle to get it moving again. Ocean tides never stop. Never. So the ocean never has to work up enough strength to build a wave and move a current. It is simply the byproduct of its nature and flows seamlessly. Love should be the same way. But if you've been waiting for that guy, that relationship or to be married to know love, then there's probably a dam between you and the other side of love that's blocking the flow. That dam can be broken by simply starting somewhere. Here are a few ideas to get it flowing again or flowing for the first time.

Send an anonymous card to a lady in the church. Put together a few blessing bags to keep in your car for the homeless in the area. Pay for the person behind you in the drive-thru and leave a note about how much God loves them. Take someone to lunch after church that you know would otherwise go home alone. Give in the special offering at church to support a missionary project. Call someone just to tell them you were thinking about them and offer to pray for them. Text someone and tell them to have a good day. Bake cookies for your team at work. Go to the nursing home and read to the elderly. It can be as simple or as grand as God puts on your heart and you're willing to listen, but begin to love someone without the expectation of anything in return.

When we love from a place of being loved, we are free to love more authentically and generously. We won't fear burn out, rejection or not being loved in return. We can begin to love in small things and in big things. In return, our lives become that conduit of love from God to others and we are loved fully in the process. So go love and love big.

"

you took me in
and made me
yours.

PSALM 27:10 TPT

Abba,

Long before the sound of Your voice brought this world into existence, Your mind was already on me. Your heart chose me as the focus of Your love and that by Your love I would be whole. You signed my adoption papers before I was even born, bringing me into Your family though Jesus. You were the proudest Dad planning all this, and simply because You wanted me in on all Your goodness (Ephesians 1:3-8). Let me never forget that You chose me. You chose me as special. I didn't amount to much, but in You I am now something. I was rejected, but no more, because in You I am accepted (1 Peter 2:9-10).

You are present with me, singing songs over me, that bring my anxiety to peace by the rescue of Your love (Zephaniah 3:17). Because You are a Father to me, I am a daughter to You (2 Corinthians 6:18). And here, You and me, us together, this is what You had in mind from the beginning (Galatians 3:26).

I know my adoption is a sealed deal because You gave me the Holy Spirit and by Him we have this beautiful connection and intimacy of words and life. What joy I have to sit at Your table, no longer trying to overhear from the next room. I can freely enjoy You and Your spread before me because You have invited me in to all that is Yours (Galatians 4:5-7).

You are a such good Father to me. I am simply overwhelmed by Your love (1 John 3:1).

So grateful I am Yours,

Daughter

Chapter Six: Protecting Purity

My mom has one of the best recipes for oatmeal chocolate chip cookies. They are so good I even eat them for breakfast. I mean, they totally have oatmeal in them. That counts, right? I also enjoy them for lunch and dinner and well, all day. They sound so good I may just pause and go bake some right now. As we go into this chapter, I wish I could invite you over to share in the warmth and smell of my cookie indulgence. Milk and cookies just seem to make the hard things softer.

I remember back to the very first time I tried my hand at baking her cookies. Epic fail! There was runny cookie dough all over the pan, spilling over into the inside of the oven and smoke billowing from the kitchen. This erupted into my frantic attempts to get the cookie sheets out of the oven. Outside they went to clear the terrible smell from the house as more dough dripped a pathway from the kitchen to the back patio. It was terrible.

My Grammy lived with us at the time and she came in to see what all the fuss was about. I was ashamed at my botched batch of cookie perfection and explained to her that I had followed the recipe exactly; I just didn't include the oatmeal.

She laughed in an endearing way and explained why the oatmeal was important to this recipe and that I couldn't just leave it out because I wanted to. Lesson learned. I am glad for it because I have continued to make that recipe for twenty-plus years and it has been a treat for so many along the way, oatmeal and all.

Purity is the nitty-gritty stuff to our lives like oatmeal is to my cookies. I've since learned to appreciate the taste and texture it brings to my mom's cherished recipe. I've also come to appreciate the value of purity in my walk as a young woman in a society that tells me I don't really need it.

We can have a lot of things right but if we are missing a primary ingredient our lives are going to get much messier than we ever anticipated. We can be honest, generous, loving, even loyal and kind. But without purity we're missing an ingredient that helps bind all the other good stuff together.

Maybe you've made a few batches in your life that have failed as badly as my first attempt at my momma's cookies, maybe even worse. Pour some milk because we still have the recipe. We can make another batch today and as long as we don't leave anything out, it will turn out far better this time around.

What Is Purity and Why Is It So Important?

I love looking up words in the dictionary. I also thoroughly enjoy reading scripture in several different translations. I believe both types of study offer a deeper understanding beyond how I might have read it or understood it before. So let's start with some definitions of "purity" from Dictionary.com and a few scriptures that support them.

1. Freedom from anything that debases (reduce in quality or value), contaminates, pollutes, etc.

    "So put to death the sinful, earthly things lurking within you. Have nothing to do with sexual immorality, impurity, lust, and evil desires. Don't be greedy, for a greedy person is an idolater, worshiping the things of this world." Colossians 3:5 NLT

2. Freedom from any admixture or modifying addition.

    "...you are not to associate with anyone who claims to be a believer yet indulges in sexual sin, or is greedy, or worships idols, or is abusive, or is a drunkard, or cheats people. Don't even eat with such people." 1 Corinthians 5:11 NLT

3. Freedom from guilt or evil; innocence.

    "Everything is pure to those whose hearts are pure. But nothing is pure to those who are corrupt and unbelieving, because their minds and consciences are corrupted." Titus 1:15 NLT

4. Physical chastity; virginity.

    "God's will is for you to be holy, so stay away from all sexual sin." 1 Thessalonians 4:3 NLT

5. Freedom from foreign or inappropriate elements.

    "You say, "Food was made for the stomach, and the stomach for food." (This is true, though someday God will do away with both of them.) But you can't say that our bodies were made for sexual immorality. They were made for the Lord, and the Lord cares about our bodies." 1 Corinthians 6:13 NLT

The dictionary is not a faith-based book and yet notice how so many of the definitions for purity begin with the word freedom. You don't need freedom from something unless you are bound by it.

I would suggest then, that the opposite of purity using the same definitions and scriptures would be:

A reduced quality of life, contaminated and polluted by the things of this world.

Modifying our understanding of scripture by mixing with those who don't live by what it says and who worship other gods or religions.

Guilt-ridden. Having lost our innocence by a corrupted conscience having not believed in the Word of God.

Participating in sexual sin.

Plagued by sexual immorality in the same way disease is foreign to our bodies because it doesn't belong.

This is why protecting your purity is so important.

Your spirit, soul, mind and body were made for purity. You were created guiltless, blameless, righteous and innocent. Purity should be the thread woven across our entire lives, in attitude and thoughts, in heart and deed, in life and faith, in relationships and with other believers. You weren't built to sustain guilt or carry immorality. You were made to clearly understand the Word of God and to apply His heart of love in truth to every area of your life.

Yet we involve ourselves in things we can't involve Him in and by this we contaminate that area of our lives and diminish the quality of life He intended for us to experience.

> "How can a young man stay pure? Only by living in the
> Word of God and walking in its truth." Psalm 119:9 TPT

So how do we get back to the quality of life He designed without all the compromise and guilt when we live in a world dominated by immorality? By running.

Run from… ....

Paul tells Timothy to "RUN from anything that stimulates youthful lusts" (2 Timothy 2:22 NLT, emphasis added). Think about that. Anything that causes him to lust, his immediate reaction should be to RUN. Most of us probably dwell on it for a second, drink it in, soak it up, talk about it, and then decide if we're going to act on it.

At least this is what I do when I'm headed for a second helping of ice cream, or another one of those cookies. My first reaction when I come across something that is pleasing to me that I desire, whether good or bad, is not to slam the freezer door or close the cookie jar and exit the kitchen with a bottle of water. Nope. I stand there just looking at that Breyer's Rocky Road until I've let all the cold air out of the freezer. Sometimes I don't even think about it; I just grab it without a second thought.

We were born with a sin nature but we have to realize that thing died when we became a new creation in Christ Jesus (2 Corinthians 5:17). We can no longer identify with our old habits, desires and choices that Jesus paid a high price on the Cross to set us free. We must identify ourselves with who we now are in Christ, so that anything that proves contrary would raise caution in our hearts not to partake.

If I constantly think of myself as still being a sinner, I will do what sinners do, sin. If I constantly think of myself as a daughter of God, redeemed and made new, I will do what my Daddy does and live in holiness.

Temptation is going to come and our best outcome will come if we run from it. But you won't run, not if you haven't made up in your mind the areas that are no-go for you. You will contemplate, reason, think about, weigh options, and in the heat of the moment, you'll most likely give in. You will fold because you can always find a good enough reason or excuse for what you have already decided.

Here's another chick flick reference to illustrate my point. A girl is on location for her job in Paris and, of course, is caught up in the romance of the city. Coincidentally, she runs into a work acquaintance and he begins making advances that she is flattered by, but feels she can't entertain.

She starts off great by listing out all the reasons she shouldn't sleep with him. My thoughts: *("Yes! Go girl!")*. First, she's recently broken up with her boyfriend *("Rebound, hello?")*, she's already had too much to drink *("Uh-huh, not smart!")*, that she's in Paris *("romantic city, girl, I get it. But no!")*. She goes on to say they had just met *("You have no idea who this guy really is!")*. She ends by saying she's out of excuses *("You already listed plenty of good ones!")*. Unfortunately, the next scene they wake up together in bed.

All her reasons made a great case to not sleep with the guy. But in the end, she didn't listen to any of her own advice. It's a theatrical case to make a point that your best reasoning won't excuse you from what you're lusting for, if you have not made up your mind already what is most important.

Did you hear me talking to her? But did she listen? Of course she didn't because she couldn't hear me, but you can hear you and I'm sure you have gut instincts more often than you might admit. You just might not be listening to them whole-heartedly yet. For your sake, start listening to that inner voice that reminds you of your value, your boundaries and your true heart's desire over your current temptation! Is it going to diminish your quality of life or bring things into the mix that cause confusion? Will it cause guilt or shame or rob innocence? Is it foreign to how you were created to live and be?

Running should become a knee-jerk reaction, an automatic default, your first instinct and immediate response. The longer you wait to decide, the case against good judgement begins to falter. Be alert, be aware and define no-go areas. Temptations will come, but you won't run as long as those areas of your heart remain undefined or you continue to ignore your conscience, when it is trying to give you a way out!

This is a great time to set some boundaries around your heart. Be a protector of your purity. Partner your soul with God and His Word and work out what your triggers are. What are your no-go areas? Seek accountability through His Word and through Godly friends or mentors. We talk more about this in the "Developing Discipleship" chapter. This step takes you to an increased level of growth and maturity without all the try-and-fail-and-try-again.

Run To...

Protecting purity isn't just about running away from what the Holy Spirit and Scripture are telling you is wrong. It is also about running towards an alternative that will reap far better rewards than if you give into whatever you are desiring. In the same chapter, Paul encourages Timothy "to pursue righteous living, faithfulness, love, and peace and to enjoy the companionship of those who call on the Lord with pure hearts" (2 Timothy 2:22 NLT).

This means you won't remain pure by default; you must choose it. What you think about, what you watch, what you listen to, who your friends are, the places you go, the conversations you allow yourself to take part in are all choices. You also must choose purity in your dream life, including the dreams you choose, dwell on and even create through your own hopes and fantasies.

Take for an example, Joseph (Genesis 37-50). He rose to the top no matter the situation. Yeah, he had some low blows; he was rejected by his brothers, sold as a slave, extradited to a foreign land, accused of rape, wrongly imprisoned and then forgotten about for years. But they didn't seem to keep him down for very long. And when down, he could have had the attitude that he had been through so much he deserved whatever seemingly good thing came his way. So, when his boss' wife pursued him over-and-over again, he most definitely could have come up with good enough reason to justify sleeping with her. However, he had resolved in his heart that his purity was deeply connected to his relationship with God and it simply wasn't worth it.

> "She kept putting pressure on Joseph day after day, but he refused to sleep with her, and he kept out of her way as much as possible. One day, however, no one else was around when he went in to do his work. She came and grabbed him by his cloak, demanding, "Come on, sleep with me!" Joseph tore himself away, but he left his cloak in her hand as he RAN from the house." (Genesis 39:10-12 NLT, emphasis added)

Our choices seem to hinge on that one date, that one night, that special someone, that moment, that video, that friend. All of that fades quickly and then you're left with the outcome of whatever you chose. There are consequences that last much longer than the temporary pleasure of giving into what is tempting you to compromise. It's physical, emotional, spiritual, and the cons will always outweigh the pros when you choose to give in. But the pros far outweigh the cons when you choose to RUN!

Joseph was a pretty smart guy! What made him so smart? Glad you asked. First, he "kept out of her way as much as possible." Sometimes our battles would be fewer if we didn't go looking for them. Second, he "ran from the house." I wish I could say he was taking my advice to RUN, but since that's not possible, let's just say we got our tips from the same "Source."

On a flip side, think about what he would have given up had he given into a persistent temptation. In that moment, he would have lost his job, one where he had worked his way to the top. He was a slave, so he probably would have been killed. But there were other things on the line. Joseph's life counted for more than just his life; the salvation of an entire nation from seven years of famine, his dad's life, his brother's lives, the welfare of the Egyptian nation and the destiny of the Israelites all rested on Joseph. His fortitude to walk with God and not sleep with a woman that knocked on his door every day was a choice that could have cost him his destiny and the futures of millions more!

Joseph didn't know millions of people were hanging in the balance, though, because his temptation came before his influence grew. You may not think your life counts for much right now, but girl, it does! Your life, including your choices, count for far more than you could ever realize this side of eternity.

He chose purity over Potiphar's wife. He chose integrity over entitlement when wrongfully imprisoned. He chose humility over selfishness by serving others even while he was suffering. He chose to honor God over himself when he told Pharaoh his dream. He chose forgiveness over hatred by not condemning his brothers for all they had done, though by then he legally could have.

Joseph chose purity in every area of his life. We choose, too. We choose in every situation. At every crossroads, the direction of our lives is nothing more than our choosing. Even when we are handed terrible situations, it's how we handle ourselves that determines our path ahead!

Maybe there are a couple of areas that are looming at the doorway to your soul and never seem to give you any rest. No matter what is luring you to compromise, a new job, a new boyfriend, or a new best friend, lust, greed or pride; it won't satisfy and the temptation will continue and even grow. This is an invitation to devotional study and prayer closet time with the One that already defeated every foe on your behalf. Partner with Him to bring His victory into your life and defeat the desires in your heart that have tempted you to stay instead of RUN.

Okay girl, can we just go there for a minute? Let's just grin and bear it, because it's probably going to get a little uncomfortable and totally awkward, but I know that it will be worth it. Could totally use a batch of those cookies right about now.

I get it. Sexual longing is super frustrating because you can't do anything about it. To give into any sort of sexual pleasure, outside of a covenant marriage with your husband, is wrong and will bring a world of delusion and perversion in your life. Instead of giving into those thoughts, feelings or urges, resolve to stand up for yourself and break out of those traps before you dwell in and act on them. If certain thoughts or dreams come, change your course of thought. If watching a couple kiss in a movie activates something inside of you, turn away, better yet – go refill your drink.

You are worth keeping your sexual desire asleep until perfect love comes to awaken it. Don't awaken it before you are able to respond in love through covenant (Song of Solomon 2:7, 3:5, 8:4). Don't awaken it with your thoughts, self-pleasure, a boyfriend, the fantasies that play in your mind, pornography or entertainment. You don't have to live constantly frustrated because you allow yourself to feel a certain way but can't do anything about it – or do the wrong thing. Sexual desire can remain asleep until you awaken it. So, don't awaken it. Protect purity in every area of your life and if you are tempted, run from whatever is tempting you, shake it off and set yourself to remain holy.

We are each sitting on one side or the other of the same coin. Either you've had sex or you haven't. But don't let yourself believe that just because you haven't had sex that you are pure, or just because you have, that you're a lost cause and might as well give up protecting your purity.

To the first, those who haven't. I am a thirty-something year old virgin in deed but not necessarily in thought. There have been times that I have allowed the seeds sown, mostly by scenes in movies (not porn, just regular PG-13 rated movies) to replay in my own mind under the context of "when I'm married." But just because this hasn't played out in a physical act, doesn't mean I'm not an adulterer at heart (Matthew 5:28). I may not have had sex yet, but there have been times when making out in some guy's car made me feel cheapened and less valued. My virginity got sweeter with time and held greater value the longer I held onto it. The shame and regret that would come, if I ever gave myself out of marriage, wasn't worth even the most romantic moment.

God had to heal me in the heart area because of the thoughts I had allowed to play in my dreams. You cannot unsee what you see or unhear what you hear outside of the grace and power of the Blood of Christ. Images from movies would flash back and haunt me, replaying without notice and causing shame and loneliness. The enemy knows where we are weak and, like the sick and perverted thing that he is, plays on those weaknesses until we break. But you don't have to break!

Remember earlier when I shared about giving up TV and movies? Well, those flashback images went away completely. Not watching anything removed even the slightest influence to allow the enemy to magnify any image in the video reel of my mind. Not saying that you have to give up TV or movies, but if you're struggling, it can't do anything but help!

The story in Luke 7 of the lady that poured the fragrance on Jesus' feet hit me like a ton of bricks. She was a well-known sinner that entered a religious meeting where she was not welcome, in order to pour out her love on a man she had no right to be near, in gratitude for something He had not yet done. Of course, the do-gooders were appalled at her abandon of dignity and mocked her devotion. In response, Jesus tells a story comparing debts of someone who owed a lot of money and someone who owed only a little. Both were equally forgiven of their debt and it was cancelled. Turns out that the one who was forgiven the most, loved more in return out of gratitude.

We have all been forgiven much. Maybe I haven't messed up as badly as that lady with all her baggage, but being a virgin doesn't save me from the sin in my own heart. I used to hold on to it like a trophy, at least this was mine. But trophies are gods and gods exalted make me not only an adulterer at heart, but an idol worshiper as well, and my own "righteousness" became a wall between me and God. But thanks for the grace of God that rescued me from the isolation of my own religious darkness!

I encourage you to come before His presence and reconnect to His heart for your purity. Lay down the "I have's" and the "I have nots" before him and surrender the most vulnerable place of your heart, those places that hide in darkness. Surrender to him your shame, your thoughts, your dreams, your body, the times you've watched and listened to things you shouldn't, pleased yourself or gone too far. He knows it all and loves you still. Freedom comes when you bring darkness into the light and no longer allow the enemy to hold it against you. Put yourself in that lady's shoes, covered in sin and shame, she bowed at the feet of Jesus and poured out her all. He can only restore that which we surrender to him. Surrender much and allow His love to forgive you much.

To the latter, I am sorry. God created rules and boundaries about sex because He sees the value behind the way He created it to function. I am sorry that you have had to deal with the consequences of pursuing intimacy outside of covenant and joining yourself to someone who was not yours. I cannot imagine the grief that comes and inevitably ensues once you are torn from that person, when the relationship ends and the heart that grows cold when it becomes a recurring theme.

I get it. It's tough. We live in a culture that is inundated by sex, lust, pornography, exploitation of men and women, instant gratification, self-pleasing and self-indulgence. It is a constant feast of the lust of the flesh out there, and it takes some serious effort to guard against tasting to see if it's really all that bad. The world can only show us the level of love that it knows. If we don't know any different, we will follow its example. You cannot undo deeds done, but the blood of Jesus breaks every chain, even unhealthy emotional ties, and can put desire back to sleep for you until the time is right.

A story about another woman comes to mind. This time, she is a woman at a well. Jesus speaks to her, outside of custom, and calls out her value. After a brief conversation, He makes it plain that she had been married five times and wasn't married to the man she was living with. She runs back to her people and says this, "Come and see a man who told me everything I ever did," (John 4:28-30 NLT), but declared it without shame. He took away her shame and she was healed by coming face to face with a Savior that no sin can outweigh.

If you've already had sex, restoration is still a promise and comes by repentance that leads you away from doing it again (2 Corinthians 7:10). Doing what we know is wrong and then saying "sorry" leads to spiritual death resulting in a hard heart and insensitivity to the things of God. Much like in life, when you are in a real relationship with God, you will care about His perspective on your choices.

I encourage you to repent for meeting a right need the wrong way. God is ready to fill every low place and He is ready still. Bring before Him your times of compromise and partnership with lies that you've believed that it was okay to give yourself away. Put the relationships, the partnerships, the ties that were made before Him and ask forgiveness for having done things your own way instead of being obedient to His word. Then ask that He break every chain and every tie that was made and surrender your heart to Him solely.

In all sincerity, it won't look pretty when the Holy Spirit begins to go deep into your heart, memories and emotions. Just like a surgeon needs to access the wound before he can mend it, you may feel discomfort and even some pain, but then He'll touch every broken place and heal you without scars. He will restore hope in you for every promise He has spoken over you.

Along with repentance is an uphill battle that few will be vulnerable enough to share with sincerity. Sin in any form will always rob, kill and destroy. This goes deeper than you can imagine and into areas you never would have thought would be impacted by the sin you entertained. But the devil doesn't play fair. If you give him a peep hole, he is going to take over much more. Depression, addiction, disease and unhealthy emotional ties are just some of what is sown into our lives when we give into his devices.

God has put this boundary in place to protect us and save us from these weapons the enemy uses against us. I encourage you to honor God and honor your future husband. Honor the covenant of marriage, and value yourself.

Establish No-Go Areas...

So two sides of the same coin, but we all can start fresh today! We can begin to make a fresh batch of cookies, oatmeal and all. In some way, we've all messed up and fallen short. By repentance our past is washed clean and we have a clean start. For today and all your tomorrows ahead, here are some ideas to get started back on a path of sexual purity, but don't stop with these. Really dig in and write some out for yourself.

Again, purity is more than just sex, so include those no-go areas that tempt you in any area. Maybe it's watching fitness videos, fashion blogs, makeup video bloggers. Maybe you go to the gym way too often, are over-committed at work, or stay up way too late at night.

Here are a few for sexual purity; then, continue with the boundaries you know you need to set. Be honest with yourself and where you are. Hugging, kissing, snuggling, and even holding hands introduced too early, too often or too serious can be detrimental to your stand for purity.

> Laying down in bed together.
> Watching a movie alone at home in the dark.
> Heavy touching or taking off clothes.
> Watching kissing.
> Watching bedroom scenes.
> Reading relationship magazines.
> Reading articles about sex and relationships.
> Reading books with sexual themes.
> Reading pornography through novels or chapters of a book.
> Lyrical pornography in music that vividly depicts sexual themes.
> Listening to music that entices relationship thoughts.
> Allowing or encouraging fantasies with the opposite sex.
> Allowing or encouraging fantasies of sexual acts or leading up to.
> Engaging in or listening to conversations about others' sex lives.
> Hanging out with married couples who emphasize physical affection.
> Hanging out with single (and even married) men.

The easiest way to misuse something is not understanding its purpose. My dad used to use the illustration that a key can be used to open a paint can, but will most likely bend and ruin the key, because that wasn't what it was made to do.

Your body has the ability to have sex. Your life will have influence. Your stomach is built to consume food. Your soul has emotions. Your flesh seeks comfort. Your identity seeks approval and affirmation. Your life wants to be noticed. But any of these, outside of their purpose, will become abused and dysfunctional and will result in much more harm than good.

If you don't know the answer to the purpose behind your purity, you likely won't stay pure. Just like if you don't know the purpose of a diet, you won't stick to a meal plan or fitness routine.

So, what's the benefit to being pure?

> "The Lord loves those whose hearts are holy, and he is the friend of those whose ways are pure." Proverbs 22:11 TPT

The pure in heart have the unique privilege to see God (Matthew 5:8), to know Him genuinely, to experience the nearness of His presence, to walk in intimate friendship. This is why Jesus brought us to the revelation that purity isn't just in deed but truly a matter of the heart (Matthew 5:27-28). It's when sin dwells in the reservoirs of our heart that our life becomes defiled (Matthew 15:18-19). These desires then tempt us to sin and sin leads to death, separating our intimacy with the Father (James 1:15). Living a life that protects purity means our desires stay connected to our relationship with God. We are then no longer tempted by things that would harm this relationship because the desire no longer lives with us.

Remaining pure also has two sides but comes in opposite order. The hard precedes the good. You have to make the hard choice first and then reap the reward later. The world will give you its reward first and then makes you pay later.

Here are some verses that may help as you dig deeper into what God says about purity and how to walk it out in your life. I encourage you to read through them, pray through them, find areas you are strong in and celebrate them. Find areas you are weak in and things you can focus on to strengthen them. His Word is a mighty tool to help restore and uphold a life of purity in every area.

"Don't let anyone under pressure to give in to evil say, "God is trying to trip me up." God is impervious to evil, and puts evil in no one's way. The temptation to give in to evil comes from us and only us. We have no one to blame but the leering, seducing flare-up of our own lust. Lust gets pregnant, and has a baby: sin! Sin grows up to adulthood, and becomes a real killer." James 1:13-15 MSG

"There's more to sex than mere skin on skin. Sex is as much spiritual mystery as physical fact. As written in Scripture, "The two become one." Since we want to become spiritually one with the Master, we must not pursue the kind of sex that avoids commitment and intimacy, leaving us more lonely than ever—the kind of sex that can never "become one." There is a sense in which sexual sins are different from all others. In sexual sin we violate the sacredness of our own bodies, these bodies that were made for God-given and God-modeled love, for "becoming one" with another. Or didn't you realize that your body is a sacred place, the place of the Holy Spirit? Don't you see that you can't live however you please, squandering what God paid such a high price for? The physical part of you is not some piece of property belonging to the spiritual part of you. God owns the whole works. So let people see God in and through your body." 1 Corinthians 6:16-20 MSG

"God wants you to live a pure life. Keep yourselves from sexual promiscuity. Learn to appreciate and give dignity to your body, not abusing it, as is so common among those who know nothing of God. God has called us to live holy lives, not impure lives." 1 Thessalonians 4:3-5, 7 MSG

"Don't you realize that those who do wrong will not inherit the Kingdom of God? Don't fool yourselves. Those who indulge in sexual sin, or who worship idols, or commit adultery, or are male prostitutes, or practice homosexuality, or are thieves, or greedy people, or drunkards, or are abusive, or cheat people—none of these will inherit the Kingdom of God. Some of you were once like that. But you were cleansed; you were made holy; you were made right with God by calling on the name of the Lord Jesus Christ and by the Spirit of our God." 1 Corinthians 6:9-11 NLT

"Don't copy the behavior and customs of this world, but let God transform you into a new person by changing the way you think. Then you will learn to know God's will for you, which is good and pleasing and perfect." Romans 12:2 NLT

I know that was heavy. Thanks for sticking with me. God wants His very best for you and me. That's why God put it on my heart to write you this book. If no one else reads it, you are, and that counts! Your life is so beautiful and such a treasure. You, by nature, look like your Father God. He made you to look like Him! You carry in your beauty the very image of your true Father. While you are here, the enemy just wants to taint and tarnish it to hide your resemblance of God as much as he can. That's why he introduced sin to Eve in the first place. At some point, she believed God was holding out on her, so she gave in to a lesser version than God's best, the enemy's counterfeit.

God isn't holding out on you. His boundaries are for your benefit, to protect you. His Word is for your strength. His promises are for your hope. His example is for your faith. Grab hold of purity for all it truly is and let go of anything that looks like a counterfeit. It's not too late and you can do it! It'll be worth it! Begin again with Him today!

Momma's Oatmeal Chocolate Chip Recipe

1 cup Margarine
1 cup Brown Sugar
1 cup Granulated Sugar
2 Eggs
1 teaspoon Vanilla
1 teaspoon Salt
1 ½ teaspoon Baking Soda
2 cups Flour
2 cups Quick Oats Oatmeal
1 cup Chocolate Chips

Beat until fully blended after each step:
Soften margarine.
Add sugars.
Add eggs and vanilla.
Add flour, salt and baking soda.
Add oatmeal.
Add chocolate chips.

Drop by tablespoon onto greased baking sheet. Bake at 325° for 10 to 12 minutes or until slightly golden brown.

Chapter Seven: Why I Am Waiting

I mentioned in the previous chapter that I was a virgin. Being that I am in my thirties I understand that this has become far more rare than it used to be. Even still, I know there are many of you who have your heart set to remain pure and wait until marriage to have sex. I also know that statistically many of you already have and that most of you wish you had waited longer. I never had a birds-and-bees talk with my parents. No one ever shared with me step-by-step from Scripture God's perspective on sex. It was just a big "No." No. We don't talk about it. No. Don't do it. No. It's a sin. I knew "no" but I didn't understand why until long after I had decided to guard my heart by waiting to share it completely.

I wanted to take a moment to share my heart with you because I know this is a battle we often fight alone. Some of the questions can be embarrassing, so though magazines and blogs provide answers, how do you really know if they can be trusted? We don't want to judge or come off as judgmental, so having the purity talk with friends is even hard. Even asking ladies at church can be awkward at best, so we find it better to avoid it all together. So we end up alone, trying to navigate a mine field of pressure coming from all angles, with good intentions of making the right choices, but feeling helpless in really knowing how. So how do you know what the line is? Where do you draw it in today's culture? What if you've already passed it?

There are many stories of girls who have already had sex but later wish they hadn't, and I am thankful for their voice, but do we really hear them? Maybe you've heard it before but didn't really believe how much they regretted it, thought your relationship would be different or simply wanted to go it your own way and hope for the best. I'd like to tell you there is more than hoping for the best! From a 30+ single girl who's not socially awkward or plain weird, waiting to have sex has been one of the best on-going decisions of my life and I see the fruit of this in so many areas of my life. I'm sure I'll understand the benefits even more, once I'm married, but I'm already benefitting.

> "If only I had listened to wisdom's voice and not stubbornly demanded my own way, because my heart hated to be told what to do!" Proverbs 5:12 TPT

We don't like being told that sex isn't a good idea. We see it portrayed with such glamorous and romantic appeal, how could it really be as destructive as the old ladies at church say? Not only that, but it has become exceedingly more common. When it's in almost every movie, tv show, song and conversation at school or work, how can we be expected to be *different* than "everyone else who is doing it"?

We listen. We listen to wisdom's voice and not demand our own way. We allow our minds to be transformed into the way that God thinks. Your best will always and forever be wrapped up in God's unending and never changing love for you. This is the same love that gave us the Bible, which includes the boundaries about sex.

So, why am I waiting?

First, Obedience to God

When I read my Bible I hear His heart for my success and well-being. When Wisdom (Jesus) tells me not to lie, steal, gossip or lust, I can read further to see how it benefits me to obey. There are *always* promises attached to obedience and consequences to disobedience. We sing about His promises in songs at church, but we can't walk in them unless we live according to how He designed our lives to function.

Proverbs 5 is a great read on this topic, and especially in the Passion Translation.

God doesn't want your years to be squandered – by a tormented conscious as a result of sin (5:9). He doesn't want the scars of your own conscience to become the ropes that tie you up (5:22). He doesn't want pieces of you to die for lack of self-control (5:23). He doesn't want you to be robbed of your destiny (5:23). You were never built to carry a bitter conscience (5:4). You were never made to feel the sting of sin piercing your soul like a sword (5:4).

You were made to know love (5:15). You were designed to be truly loved, like how He first loved us, completely unconditional and selfless. Sex does not equal love and sex outside of marriage is quite the opposite, short-sighted and selfish. God created sex and all that He created was good. But we only experience His goodness when we live according to the patterns and boundaries that He established.

So I am waiting to have sex because my obedience is worth all of His promises that I get in return.

We cannot hope to walk in His blessing when we traverse our own path. "He sees everything you do and his eyes are wide open." This isn't a scary mean-dad thing… this is a good Father who says "I love you so much I am going to continually pursue you with Perfect Love and give you a chance at a way out so that you don't have to go down this path. I want my light to hit your every dark place. My love to fill every low place. My identity to rewrite every label. My grace to remove every shame. Everything twisted by sin is a counterfeit to something I created that was good. Return to my good for you. Trust that it is better than anything the world could offer (Psalm 139:11-12, 1 Corinthians 10:13, Psalm 119:64, 1 Peter 2:9, Isaiah 54:4, 3 John 1:11).

He desires a relationship for you that has love without strings. Sex without shame. Intimacy without rejection. Vulnerability without exposure. Truth drenched in love. I encourage you to read Proverbs 5 with an open heart to hear God's best for you about sex, which is meant to be anything but common (5:19).

MoralRevolution.com is a great resource for those that would like to read further on this topic or to find help and healing. If you are waiting, just know girl, you are not alone! And if you haven't, but feel the tug of God on your heart, begin today!

Second, to Honor the Man that Becomes My Husband.................

How I conduct my life and steward my body will become the gift I give to my husband (1 Corinthians 7:1-4). If I have sex with anyone else, I am bringing them into my marriage bed with me.

To honor the man that will become my husband, I choose to not have sex with anyone else. He, by choosing me, is worthy of the best I can offer him! So many times, we make decisions based on our own needs, wants and desires. The choice to have sex not only impacts your life but also the guy you sleep with and your future husband. Seeing that our decisions have further impact beyond the moment will help us make better decisions.

To put it frankly, you are having sex with someone else's husband. He's having sex with someone else's wife. Even though many have fallen prey, we know that adultery is wrong. What many of us have failed to see is that we commit adultery, even if we aren't married yet. No matter how casual or serious your relationship with him, until you have made a covenant before God and man – he is not yours and you are not his. Sex is a gift for those who have given themselves one to each other in covenant.

> "Let marriage be held in honor among all, and let the marriage bed be undefiled, for God will judge the sexually immoral and adulterous." Hebrews 13:4 ESV

Third, Because I Value Myself...

I put this last because if it were first, I would have probably already given in.

As girls, we easily sacrifice ourselves for the sake of others. This is a God-given gift that is beautiful, a picture of His nature and mirror of His character. We are willing to do whatever it takes to help a friend, neighbor or even a stranger in need.

But this can be to our detriment, when outside of the plans and purposes of God. Our guy will say, "I love you" and we will believe it. We have a desperate need in the foundational core of our souls to be loved and to love. This was sown into our nature by the hands of our loving Father so we would continue to pursue God and His affection for us. But when we do not seek this from God first, we will look for it in a relationship and will likely find a version of it. So in response we will reply, "I love you, too." With the mutual agreement of love and affection comes the expectation and desire to see it fulfilled.

When we do not feel loved by God and loved by others, we will seek it out wherever we can find it. This will likely develop an unhealthy relationship that will lead us into sacrificing self, for the sake of them. Meaning, he will say "if you love me..." and so we will give in so that we do not lose what we worked so hard to find.

This is why I would have probably given in already if obedience to God and honoring my future husband were not more important to me. There have been times in my life I have been desperately lonely. I have felt the aching need to be wanted, desired, loved and cared about. These unmet for too long and our souls get very unhealthy. I have lived weeks, months and even seasons in this place.

But even in the darkest seasons of my life where I didn't feel loved even by God, I knew sex was not the answer. There was always a prevailing thought that "it will end." I believe this was God's grace to save me from meeting a right need the wrong way. I always looked to what would happen on the other side of sex, and I was never convinced it was worth it. That night will end. You will have to get up and out of that bed and continue on with your life. That guy may or may not go with you, even for a day much less 'till death, but you will carry your tie with him forever. You will always wonder about him, think about him, have recurring images of him. He will have become a part of you.

By giving in, we make it even harder to not give in again. Song of Solomon calls it awakening love (Song of Solomon 2:7). Once awakened, it fills us. This is great in marriage, but detrimental if not.

Once we partake, sin will reign in our bodies making it difficult to abstain from its passions (Romans 6:12-14), which is why sin leads to greater sin. God has made us stewards of our bodies. They are not actually ours, neither is our money, time, gifts or talents. Everything belongs to God (1 Corinthians 6:19-20)!

Value of self would also refrain from self-gratification or masturbation. These acts will increase your sexual appetite while not satisfying it for very long. God created sex for the union of a man and woman in covenant, so self-gratification contradicts this design.

If we feed our souls romance, sexually themed films or books, masturbation or sexually active relationships, we are inviting a greater dependence on the fulfillment of our need before its proper time.

So why am I waiting? Because I desire to be obedient to God out of His love for me, because my future husband is going to be amazing and fully worth getting the best of me in every area, and because I value me and my body.

Now your turn. Think about God's Word, your life and my story. I hope this has helped answer some lingering questions and hopefully pushed you over the edge into the steadfast walk of purity. So… why are you waiting?

Here are a few verses if you would like to study more on this:

Exodus 20:14	1 Corinthians 5:11	Ephesians 5:3
Matthew 15:19	1 Corinthians 6:9-11	Colossians 3:5
Mark 7:20-22	1 Corinthians 6:12-20	1 Thessalonians 4:3-8
Acts 15:20	1 Corinthians10:8	Hebrews 13:4
Romans 8:4-16	2 Corinthians 12:21	Jude 1:7
1 Corinthians 5:1	Galatians 5:19-21	Revelation 21:8

For some of us, opening the door to sex wasn't a choice, but the result of abuse and force. God has restoration for you and hasn't lost sight of hope for your future! If this is you, or you are really struggling to get over current pain and life cycles, I would encourage you to seek biblical counsel from a pastor or leader in this area at your local church, who will partner with you in prayer for freedom and healing. You are not alone!

"I am waiting…"

_____

_____

_____

_____

_____

_____

_____

_____

_____

"

your ♥ for me
is so constant
& ENDLESS.

PSALM 138:8 TPT

Abba,

You'd never forget me. You just simply couldn't, because I am Yours. You're so proud to claim me that You've eternally penned my name on Your hands (Isaiah 49:16). And even though I was separated from You because of my own sin, you were thinking of me when You raised Jesus from the grave, knowing the mercy that would then pour into me by Your love (Ephesians 2:4). You proved Your love by sending Jesus, even before I could ever love You back, to eradicate my sin and the damage it did to our relationship (1 John 4:9-10).

It's crystal clear how much I am loved by You, but You didn't stop there, You put Your Father's hand of blessing on my life for something so special (1 Thessalonians 1:4).

I will fill my days singing love songs to You. I will fill the ears of those passing by of Your faithfulness. This love story, You for me – how you formed the world and secured it by the same heart that pursues me – I'll never quit telling it. Your love is the strength of my life. Your loyalty is my home (Psalm 89:1-3).

So. Much. Love. I am deeply loved by You. You are the fullness of mercy and grace, and endlessly patient with me. You always have been. Always will be (Exodus 34:6-7).

Eternally loved,

Daughter

Chapter Eight: Pursuing Adventure

A captivated life will not too quickly fall for the snares of common temptation.

Desire the experience of new. New is not daunting. New is exciting - new people, new places, new foods, new languages, new cultures, new smells, new anything. Don't let your single life wrap you up so tight in a box that you become a bore to be around, because you are waiting for that one epic adventure as the only experience of great meaning in life.

I have always had a hunger for adventure. Remember how I told you that my first flight was alone when I was only eight years old? Well, every trip since has left a mark on my life and I have a treasure in life only enhanced by each journey I've taken.

Adventure in Missions

Oh, my goodness, do I have an adventurous heart by nature and I literally crave travel! I love it! The planes, the airports, the new people, the buildings, the streets, the cultures and the way different people worship God. That one is especially one of my favorites. In all my travels, I have fallen in love with the experience of seeing His sons and daughters in places across the globe worshipping God and joining with the way they connect to the Father's heart. This is truly beautiful and life changing.

I absolutely recommend missions to every person on the planet. Get out of your comfort zone. Get out of what is familiar to you. Eat crazy foods. Sleep on terribly uncomfortable beds, or even the floor. Travel in cars that aren't fit for streets on streets that aren't fit for cars, alongside cattle, random animals, pedestrians, mopeds, motorbikes and buses. Let your hearts be touched by the children in the slums, who without Christ have no hope. Let your excitement build as you lead someone to Christ in a language you've barely learned, but know enough to share the simple Gospel. Let your heart be overwhelmed by the transformation of someone's face when they are freed from the bondage of oppression.

Get super nervous and share your testimony, your story, your moment when you met Christ and were changed forever, with a room full of wide eyes, bright smiles and hungry hearts. Share your life, your heart, your dreams, your gifts, your smile, your compassion. Share with the sick, the broken, the lost, poor and enslaved. Pour out your life into someone who will never be able to repay you. Love! Love them and you will be forever changed. Loving the people like you find on these trips is a love that even touches the heart of God! Every country is a mission. God wants to use you to deliver the Good News of His Son to people who have never heard. Every people group needs to know the love that you already possess. You need no further validation but that God's love has made you want to share it where it is unknown.

My First Mission Trip...

I didn't know how much I would love going on mission trips. I had simply attended an outdoor service in Orange County, California when Pastor Hazel Hill shared her heart about the upcoming trip to India and I felt a well spring up inside of me. I was overwhelmed and overcome by a flood of brokenness and joy in the same moment. It was like God was growing my heart. He was making it bigger to love a people I had never really considered. In that moment, I knew that her message was just for me! I lived in Mississippi and didn't know anyone going, but I signed up anyway. We ended up being a group of about fifteen women.

Landing for the first time in a third world nation, I was overcome. Compassion rose in my heart as I looked at the faces of the people; heartache then followed in seeing their condition and what their reality looked like. If I had not known the hope we were bringing, it would have been too much for me to see. Seeing the despair without having hope for a cure is unbearable.

While riding in a bus through town I caught the glimpse of some children playing in the streets. They were meagerly dressed and obviously thin.

Bouncing a soccer ball in between them, their smiles gleamed and their laughter filled the air. "They don't know they're poor," echoed in my mind. With less food, clothing and shelter than most of the people living in my nation, these children still had the ability to have fun and find enjoyment in simple things.

Along the journey we visited a sewing school and orphanage in New Delhi. I had spent the whole plane ride over putting together leather strap salvation bracelets, with the colored beads that walk you through the salvation message. It was an idea I had soon after I booked the trip. We walked through an alley way of temples and idols into a concrete brick facility. The moment those girls saw us, it was as if the world grew brighter and you could feel the sun. We met the girls and the older women who were part of the sewing school. We saw their beds and where they played. We took pictures and sang. They had a whole program ready for us. Then they got their bracelets. Oh, wow, how something so simple became so extravagant in the hands of girls who had never owned much of anything. I was flooded by joy and brokenness again. I could feel God growing my heart again. These girls were so precious and so loved by God who had rescued them, when all of life had left them abandoned, broken and alone. God was loving them through me and I felt it. I was in awe and marked forever.

I will likely never see the same girls that are now growing up to be women. Our paths will likely never cross in this life. But the hope we carried was much larger than a beaded bracelet or a song and a dance. We carried the message of Jesus into a place surrounded by poverty and oppression. The Gospel message shared becomes life and breath where no other light shines. And now, beyond the shrines and the alleys, the starving bodies and the dirty clothes, are beautiful souls who find hope only in the name of Jesus Christ. That is far worth the journey and the sacrifice, the investment and the pouring out of my heart.

Is life Unshared Only Half Enjoyed?

Long before my first mission trip, I was in my Junior year of high school and had the awesome opportunity to go to Paris, France. It was the reason I took French as my foreign language; though now, I really wish I had taken Spanish, as it would have proven to be far more useful. Even still, I boarded my first international flight with a group of my best girl friends from high school, and we flew over the Atlantic into the most romantic city I had known at the time. The old architecture, the cathedrals and bridges, the cafes and bistros, the hustle and bustle of a place far away flooded my thrill of adventure.

Our teacher had been so many times she didn't even stick with us the whole time because she had friends in the city. My dad totally freaked out when he found that out, but nevertheless it only added to our fun. I had no beau to write home about the trip or wait by the phone for his call. I didn't have a *Monte Carlo* movie experience (which came out at least a decade after) but my trip was still a blast, and I saw the Eiffel Tower sparkle in the night with my very own eyes. I looked through the glass pyramids of The Louvre and saw Mona Lisa face to face. I walked under The Arc de Triomphe and dawned the halls of Versailles with its Hall of Mirrors.

I've been to many nations all around the world and there has often been an opportunity for me to focus and enjoy the beauty of the moment alone. I sat alone in the Nigerian airport waiting to travel to Kenya to meet my next group. I didn't even realize that I was going to be alone until my family took off on their flight back to the US, and there I sat in Nigeria going to Kenya, not knowing who or when I would meet my next group. Again, that moment would have been nice to have shared with someone, but I lived! I experienced adventure I hadn't planned and courage has instilled in me independence to keep tracking across this globe, whether someone goes with me or not.

Don't let your single status rob you of taking in the beautiful moments of life - the first snowfall, the rainbow that spreads the gloomy sky after a summer shower, the smell of crisp fall air on a walk alone. Life is beautiful! There are adventures to be had and enjoyed and experienced in the fullness of life.

If you just aren't gutsy enough to go it alone, be more creative about who would like to adventure with you. It most certainly doesn't have to be a husband or even a boyfriend or best friend. Find a gal friend that enjoys the same thing you do and go with them. I have made some of the unlikeliest friends at church, who don't seem to match me at all, but I've had fun going places with them simply because we have the same hunger for trips and little adventures.

Start where you can and let your dreams grow. The world is waiting for you to get out of your box and explore its treasures.

Adventure Anywhere

You can find adventure anywhere you look. Find something to explore and explore it, like a hiking trail or a new park. Find a concert a couple of cities over, grab a few friends and do a weekend or an overnighter. Eat at a different restaurant. Join a life group at church that fits your age group or hobby. Take cooking classes. Pick up music lessons. Run a 5K. Take a road trip, short or long. Do something that expands your life into new things and new people and new places. It's exhilarating. Don't be so insecure that you may not fit in that you never try anything new. If it doesn't work or you didn't like it, at least you lived a little more than you did before you tried; you will have a story to tell, then try something new again with something else.

Look up what's going on in your city, grab a friend and go. Date nights aren't the only thing that makes up a social life. If your calendar isn't full, fill it with something adventurous and then grow in your spirit of adventure. If leaving the house is a big deal for you, then start there. If a trip is where you're at, go somewhere more exotic. If you're already super adventurous, expand your horizons or who you go with. Challenge yourself to pursue life and it will rejuvenate you and refresh you in ways that nothing else can.

Even in the Small Things

Friday and Saturday nights are the worst, right? It's like all of the sudden it feels like the rest of the world has something so cool to do and your social calendar...check again...is still empty. I don't know how many times a movie rental and pasta have made a very empty weekend night pass (not anymore, of course). I know, so lame, right? Not that people even use the term "lame" anymore, but that's such a descriptive word. Friends have dinner plans, my married friends have couple plans, my working friends are working and with no special guy, I am up to myself to fill my nights. If your calendar ever empties out, here are some ideas.

Get ready anyway! Take a shower, fix your hair and put on some make up. Go somewhere, anywhere, just get out of the house! Put on those high heels and take yourself to a local coffee shop with a book. Drink a coffee that is fun to order and breathe. Just because your social calendar isn't super exciting right now, doesn't mean that your life terrible. Sometimes you just have to learn to appreciate yourself when someone else isn't there. And if someone is and you don't know them yet, strike up a conversation. It can be simple; a comment on their shoes, what they ordered, the book they are reading…you may find a new friend just chatting at a coffee shop. If the conversation doesn't build, you haven't lost anything, just go back to reading your book.

Treat yourself to a tasty dinner at a nicer restaurant. Eating for one isn't humiliating, people do it far more often than you think. The only one that is judging you is you. Your waiter doesn't care, as long as you still leave a good tip. Take a book…not work or social media, but a book! Enjoy the time. Then walk around the mall and window shop. Or even get yourself a treat if you've got a little to spend, just be cautious that you're not dipping into retail therapy that you'll inevitably regret.

Movies are also great…and they don't have to be shared to be enjoyed. I've even learned how to enjoy going to the movies alone. Just be sure you don't feed your emotional roller-coaster with a sappy one that will make you feel more depressed when you walk out, than when you walked in… hello?! Gotta guard your heart, girl… even in practical things. If not, you'll sound like the paragraph below. So. Not. Pretty!

I remember the first movie I watched by myself in a theater. I had just moved to California and was so emotional because I was in a new place far away from familiar comfort. I hardly knew anyone, so I used online maps to find a movie theater and went by myself for the first time ever in my life. It, of course, was a pre-teen cheesy chick flick and I balled my eyes out during most of it. Not because of the movie, but because here I was feeling super low just because I was at the movies alone. Oh, how far I've come when I realized that going to the movies solo didn't mean the end of the world.

Near or far, expensive or free, in a group or alone – get creative and pursue adventure. Enlarge your capacity to enjoy the manifold treasures that lie within your grasp, if you'd but go out and search for them. Drama broods in the realm of a small world that is minimized by complacency or fear. You will rarely find drama in the lives of those whose world is largely explored and ever expanding.

And if you want to go a step even further, develop skills in order to impact the world you explore.

"

i know **YOU**
are there for me
so i will not
BE SHAKEN.

PSALM 27:3 TPT

Abba,

You are the glue that holds me together when everything seems to be falling apart. I'm depending on You because in You is all I'll ever need. If nothing else seems to be going my way, I can smile, because You have given me Your name. Your eyes are on me. Your love is for me. At the sound of my cry, You come to my rescue (Psalm 33:18-22).

You are good to me. As good as Your Word. I'm all in to do this life Your way, so I ask You to be my instructor. I was so out of step and off beat with Your Word, let Your goodness bring me back into perfect timing with You. Eyes on You, You have my focus. Let's dance to revelation's rhythm. Every misstep has brought me back to the basics, stronger each time. Following Your lead is my upmost desire (Psalm 119:65-72).

You're with me in hard times (2 Corinthians 1:4). Everything from You is good, light with no shadow, no strings attached (James 1:17). Thank you for being endlessly patient with me and not being easily angered, but rather You cover me with Your grace (Psalm 145:79). I can take You at Your Word. If You say it, You're going to do it. You keep Your promise. Every. Time. I'm eyes locked on You, expectantly anticipating the lavish generosity You pour on all who are Yours. The signature on all You do is love. You hear me when I pray sincerely, and like a good Father, always do what's best for me. My heart calls out for You!

Stick by me, I know You will (Psalm 145:13-20) because there is nothing in all of reality that can come between us. No matter what I go through, how high or low the road, it won't touch my conviction of Your love for me. I'm wrapped tight in the arms of my Savior, unmoved by anything else (Romans 8:35-39).

Trusting Your lead,

Daughter

Chapter Nine: Developing a skill

You may know the saying, "From everyone who has been given much, much will be required" (Luke 12:48 NASB). Well you have been given much. You are a steward of your life and all that your life touches. This means your eyes, your ears, your mouth, your heart, your mind, your money, your time...shall I go on? You are even a steward of this season of being single. It's not a holding area until you get on the train to take you to your next stop. It's not the rehearsal period to make you a better wife for when you get married. If you steward this season well, you will again have to choose how you will steward the next season. It will always be your choosing as to how well you handle all that God gives you in every season.

Because it matters

How you live single matters just as much as how you will live married! I'm going to say that one more time, just for effect... How you live single matters just as much as how you will live married!

The issues you have now will not suddenly go away as soon as you get married. If you struggle with devotional time now, imagine once your time is now divided with the demands of being a wife. You think it will be easier having a godly husband to encourage you, but the priorities you have now will be the priorities you take with you into your next season. Unless you develop and mature good priorities or break and uproot bad ones, they will never change.

Don't be that person that watches all of life's opportunities pass her by, because she believes in her heart that she will only accomplish great things "when I am married." What a tragedy!

Quite frankly I have enjoyed many adventures in this life already, that I would have missed completely had I waited! There is no guarantee what opportunities may or may not come down the road later, if we don't seize them now. How sad to spend life waiting only to realize you've missed it the whole time!

Think about David (1 Samuel 16-18). If you're like me, at first your mind immediately goes to David and Goliath. Well, mine used to as well but doesn't anymore. God has revealed to my heart the importance of David's season alone. Yep, alone! He was alone with those sheep in the wilderness fields for years. Years! He became accustomed to being alone and instead of wasting that time, he stewarded it well. He grew in relationship with God and he grew in skill.

How do we know this? We can look at the testimony of the Goliath experience as evidence of the stewardship of his single season.

David had such an undeniable, unwavering, unshakable faith in the God of the Israelites that He didn't flinch at the thought of taking down an enemy of the LORD. The trained armies of Israel were shaking in their boots.

> "Don't worry about this Philistine," David told Saul. "I'll go fight him!"
>
> "Don't be ridiculous!" Saul replied. "There's no way you can fight this Philistine and possibly win! You're only a boy, and he's been a man of war since his youth." But David persisted. "I have been taking care of my father's sheep and goats," he said. "When a lion or a bear comes to steal a lamb from the flock, I go after it with a club and rescue the lamb from its mouth. If the animal turns on me, I catch it by the jaw and club it to death. I have done this to both lions and bears, and I'll do it to this pagan Philistine, too, for he has defied the armies of the living God!" 1 Samuel 17:32-36 NLT

Trust isn't an overnight thing – trust is proven over time. David trusted that God would back both him and his slingshot. He saw his God beyond the enemy and knew he couldn't fail.

David played and ministered before the Lord, and before Saul, and the Lord's presence became evident (1 Samuel 16:14-23). This was only possible because David cultivated intimacy with the Lord in his alone time.

David captured the lion and the bear by the jaw and clubbed them to death in order to rescue a lamb (1 Samuel 17:34-36). Overnight success? I think not. Let me take you to the zoo and see if you would run up to a 400-pound lion and take it by its jaw and see who wins, much less one not sleepy from a sedentary life. These aren't just stories. This is our history and our very heritage. David was skilled as a worshipper, a shepherd, with a slingshot and protecting that which had been entrusted to him.

David was single and alone. Had he complained or envied his brothers, he would not have become king of Israel and the very Son of God would not have come through his lineage.

He stewarded his alone season well by maturing his relationship with God alongside developing a skill. In return, God could use what He had invested inside him during that season. This wasn't because David was special, but simply because David said, "yes."

Specifically Chosen

When I think of becoming skillful in an area, I think of the Old Testament passages when God gave instructions to build the Tabernacle, while the Israelites were traveling through the wilderness on their way to the Promised Land.

> "I have specifically chosen Bezalel son of Uri, grandson of Hur, of the tribe of Judah. I have filled him with the Spirit of God, giving him great wisdom, ability and expertise in all kinds of crafts. He is a master craftsman...I have given special skill to all the gifted craftsmen so they can make all the things I have commanded you to make." Exodus 31:1-6 NLT

How cool is that? I'm not saying they got some kind of miraculous download where they immediately knew how to do all these amazing things. If they did, most of us would write them off as "chosen" and "separate" and disassociate ourselves from the fact that God can and will do the same thing in us. I mean, maybe they did, but what if they just had an inspiration to put their hand to something and as they did God blessed it. Whether it be an instrument, a craft or a trade, it could be in a thousand different areas. God has given a unique gifting to you that matches the destiny He has for you.

Wisdom and ability and expertise may just be waiting on you to stretch out your hand and apply it to something you don't already know.

What if Edison had never tried DIY projects? He would have never become the inventor with over 1,000 patents credited to his name. What if Beethoven had never sat down to a piano or Picasso had never attempted to paint? Think of the modern advancements and art culture we would not have if the "greats" had not attempted what they did not know at one point. Great leaders didn't always influence. Great musicians had to learn scales. Great educators had to learn first. Book writers first had to read.

What is the world missing because you are…waiting? Thinking your life will finally find meaning and direction because you can now check Mrs. on an application rather than Miss is a grave misconception that will eventually disappoint. Be brave and find the courage that God has infused into your being that is needed to accomplish the greatness He has for your life. There is great fulfillment in accomplishing something bigger than yourself and beyond what you've accomplished so far. Learn an instrument, a craft or a trade…learn something more than you know now.

Will it be challenging? Yes. If it's not, dream even bigger!

Nothing Wasted

I'll tell you this, nothing I have ever ventured out to try has ever been wasted. My sister has a print out of one of the very first drawings done in an old computer program called Paint. I continued to learn and grow and try and fail and God has used that to contribute graphics design work for many churches around the globe. This helped further the Gospel and invite people into an experience with Him. From Paint. Seriously, girls, this isn't rocket science stuff here. Or maybe for you it is. Whatever it is, find it and develop it. And then do it again.

I wouldn't say my life is grand, but God has done remarkable things through me simply because of my eagerness to develop in many different areas. And there are many more to be uncovered in my life. Every area helps expand the Kingdom of God in the cities and nations where He has called me.

Just like with Bezalel, He wants to give you great wisdom, ability and expertise in all kinds of things, because He loves you and wants to enrich your life. He also loves every single person in this world and you never know when that gift will reach someone you may not have been able to reach without it.

So end procrastination! Stop putting off until tomorrow what you can do today! You don't have to wait anymore. Begin that dream, that hobby, that skill, that trip, that adventure, NOW! Whatever that is for you, stop waiting and get to it!

Discover Inspiration...

Maybe you have no idea what your gifts are or what you could do outside of what your life looks like right now. Put your feelers out there and discover new inspiration. Try and try again. Do something your friends enjoy doing and see if that sparks anything within you. If not, then try something else. You won't fail for trying. Find a class about something you don't know and take it. If you hate it, try something else. You never know what you may find that you will absolutely love and find such pleasure in doing!

To develop takes intentional effort to grow. God wants this for our lives, yes in skill, but also in our relationship with Him!

"

when you *trust* in the LORD for
FORGIVENESS
his *wrap-around*
LOVE
will *surround* you.

PSALM 32:10 TPT

Abba,

It's agony to keep it all in. My body can't contain the grief of my sin and groans for relief (Psalm 32:3-5). I come clean, open and honest, and admit my sin to You because I know You won't let me down. You're true to Your Word and forgive me (1 John 1:8-9). Thank you Jesus for being willing to carry my sin, when You had none of Your own, so I could be restored (2 Corinthians 5:21). Your eyes don't see it. Your ears can't hear it. Your heart doesn't remember the pain my sin caused. It's gone. You are better than I could ever imagine! You have kept every promise made so long ago, continuing Your merciful compassion even before Abraham until now, and beyond (Micah 7:18-20).

Your blood poured out to break the sentence of every punishment held against me for my rebellion (Ephesians 1:7). I was a dead man walking, wandering aimlessly as an outcast, but You breathed pure life back into me, bringing me into the life of your name, Jesus (Ephesians 2:6, 19).

Hate flooded and chaos pulled me under, I lost footing to the void it dug in me. I was caught in the undertow but You came to rescue me. From heaven high to sea deep, You pulled me out. Safe now, on the shore of Your love in awe to be so ardently pursued, I turn from it all to You (Psalm 18:6, 16-19).

Like a new day and fresh breath, I have a new start. Your love pursues me, goes before me and follows me.

My history rewritten,

Daughter

Chapter Ten: Developing Discipleship

We have a service at our church called Timothy. It's a discipleship group with our pastor on Sunday nights, and my life would not be the same without it. I feel that I have grown more from that one class than in all my years of being a Christian combined. How has it impacted me so greatly? Because it invites me into a deeper walk with God than I know how to go on my own. There is always a time of revelation and then application. It hurts most times. It's truly uncomfortable. I face things I didn't realize I was still dealing with or ever knew I had. I cry ugly tears and always hoard the tissue box. But I always come out of meeting God in that place more whole than I walked in.

It's in discipleship that I realized my roots of rejection. With thoughts all the way back to grade school hallways and bullies and mean words. Labels that needed removing and love to fill where rejection had robbed my identity.

It's in discipleship that family hurts came into the light so I could see them for what they really were and allow God to restore His perspective in me.

It's in discipleship he reminds me I am a daughter and that I am His. All the clichés of Christianity I grew up with soon met the reality of faith and who God really is in the ache of my loneliness and isolation.

It's in discipleship that He speaks over me, activating my purpose and grounding me in acceptance.

I have no way of more fully explaining it than with Ecclesiastes 3:2-8. Each of these have happened in discipleship at some point within areas of my heart and soul, instilling deeper trust and a more intimate walk with my Father.

A time to plant and a time to harvest.
A time to kill and a time to heal.
A time to tear down and a time to build up.
A time to cry and a time to laugh.
A time to grieve and a time to dance.
A time to scatter stones and a time to gather stones.
A time to embrace and a time to turn away.
A time to search and a time to quit searching.
A time to keep and a time to throw away.
A time to tear and a time to mend.
A time to be quiet and a time to speak.
A time to love and a time to hate.
A time for war and a time for peace. (NLT)

So in a book about Savoring Single is a chapter that could apply to everyone. We all need discipleship. From a girl raised in church, in a godly family, that served the Lord; a girl who was shielded from many of life's tragedies; a girl who was guarded well with strict rules and a conservative upbringing; let me say that I have needed discipleship more than I could have ever imagined.

Our group is normally small in comparison to the size of our church. The cost of discipleship is one many aren't ready to pay. Much like military boot camp, no one wants to do it, but I wouldn't want to go into war without it.

Being single can often feel like a war. Our emotions are in constant battle between positive and debilitating, self-worth and self-doubt. We have to guard ourselves from what other people say, guard our hearts from what we think and fight to maintain our own standard of eligibility.

I have fought this battle on my own for far too long, lost in my own despair, covered under shame and confusion. All the while there were answers and hope, help and healing. I never found it deep enough in Sunday morning attendance. I found it in discipleship.

Think about the natural processes of your body. If you don't eat, you will starve and become unhealthy. If you eat but don't expend the energy or waste, you become unhealthy. Both end in lack of health and strength for the way your body is intended to function. You need to take in and then you need to put out.

Same goes with your spirit man. Jesus said that we can't live by the natural only, but must feed on the Spirit (Matthew 4:4). But if all we do is feed, and never do, we become lazy and unhealthy Christians.

James tells us not to just listen to the Word of God, but to follow it up with action (James 1:22). This is so important. We can't just go to church week after week after week, hear a message and experience the presence of God, only to go home and do nothing about it. Nor can we rely on inspirational Scripture quotes on Instagram or thirty second sermonette clips on YouTube. There must be a process, an intake and an output.

This is what our discipleship lives should look like, having someone pour into our lives while we are pouring into someone else.

If you have accepted Christ as your Lord and Savior, even if it was just this morning, you know enough to disciple someone. You have entered into the knowledge of the love of God that paid a price you couldn't afford, to pay a debt you owed, in order that you could walk in relationship with Him. Done, that's enough! As you grow and learn, so will your capacity to disciple, but that doesn't mean wait until you have a degree, a ministry, a title or even a spouse.

There will always be someone that has gone farther than you. Likewise, there should always be someone in your life that isn't where you are yet. This way, you can continually grow and you can continually grow others.

What if Jesus didn't have the twelve disciples? What if Paul didn't have Timothy? What if Moses didn't have Joshua? What if Elijah didn't have Elisha? What if Eli didn't have Samuel?

Notice by way of Jesus' example in three subsequent chapters of Luke how Jesus' discipleship grew. In Luke 8:1, *"Jesus* began a tour of the nearby towns and villages, preaching and announcing the Good News about the Kingdom of God" (NLT). Then in Luke 9:1, "Jesus called together his *twelve* disciples and gave them power and authority to cast out all demons and to heal all diseases" (NLT). Finally, in Luke 10:1, "The Lord now chose *seventy-two* other disciples and sent them ahead in pairs to all the towns and places he planned to visit" (NLT).

There is an intentional progression in discipleship that reproduces at an exponential rate, if we follow the pattern in Scripture; first Jesus, then the twelve, then the seventy-two.

Church attendance is great, but your pastor's job isn't to be the only one that ministers, witnesses or prays for someone. It is to equip and train you to go out and do it also (Ephesians 4:12-16). Your pastor isn't there for you to feed only on his revelation of the Word. You would then spiritually starve all week because you haven't dug into the Word for yourself and are now grasping at straws for strength, until you can get back into a service to get fed again.

If it were like this in the natural, you would be very unhealthy. What if you only ate once a week? You would lose muscle mass, your bones would be weak, your immune system and all other functions would not operate properly. I am no doctor, but I know my body can't live on one meal a week. Neither can my spirit. I need the Word of God daily, His presence daily, worship daily to remain strong and vibrant in my walk with Christ.

You may not see yourself as capable yet, but as you pour into others you will grow. Discipling others challenges you to grow and keeps you on your toes. Knowing your impact on the lives of others increases the awareness of your own purpose and pushes you, not only into greater things but also past the temptation to give up when things are tough.

Also think of it the other way…What if the twelve disciples didn't have Jesus? What if Timothy didn't have Paul? What if Joshua didn't have Moses? What if Elisha didn't have Elijah? What if Samuel didn't have Eli?

Those twelve disciples certainly didn't have it all together when Jesus found them. They needed serious help. So do you. So do the souls your life is supposed to reach. If Jesus hadn't taken the time and effort to disciple, what would the church look like today? Non-existent. The same is true regarding Paul or Moses or Elijah or Samuel. Discipleship is tough and dirty and hard and sacrificial but rewarding and encouraging and refreshing, too. Nonetheless, it's needed and is the way Jesus set the example to build His church and spread the Good News of repentance and restoration.

Someone connected to your life needs what you already know, and you are specially positioned so that you can share it with them. New Christians need to be fed, nourished, encouraged, corrected and loved in truth and grace. Then when they are strong enough, they will become like you have exemplified. Just like Paul, follow me as I follow Christ (1 Corinthians 4:16, 11:1). They will then find someone to help as you are helping them.

This is the master plan for the New Testament church. No degree is required. No marital status to be reached. No minimum age. Step by step. Verse by verse. Topic by topic. Simply receive the love of God by faith and then share it with someone who doesn't know it yet.

If you're not sure where to start, you could buy a devotional book and follow along. Study through your pastor's message. Then, have a small group and teach it from your heart. Go chapter by chapter through a book of the Bible. They need you to become healthy. You need them to keep growing. The cycle of discipleship continues and life begins to invigorate your soul again because you have connected to purpose, His purpose. His only commission is now entrusted to us until the day He returns. That commission was not to go to church, get married, live a good life and retire with a 401K. Not that these aren't okay and may happen, but you have a much larger life for the taking.

"Therefore, go and make disciples of all the nations, baptizing them in the name of the Father and the Son and the Holy Spirit. Teach these new disciples to obey all the commands I have given you. And be sure of this: I am with you always, even to the end of the age." Matthew 28:19-20 NLT

Who Can You Disciple?

God has someone in your life in whom you can invest. You don't have to term it "disciple." Just be available for encouragement and support. Answer their questions with wisdom and truth over personal experience and opinion. Offer to pray with them and help them grow in the knowledge of God.

As you are reading this book, you might have had the idea to start a girls' group at your church or small group at your school, to read through this book together, discuss, pray and encourage each other. That's discipleship! If that's you, I have information and resources just for you; more information on this in the back of the book!

Who Can Disciple You?

I understand that many churches don't have what I have in our Timothy class, but every church has someone whose heart is genuinely pursuing the Father. Find this one. She may not have a title or position. She may be a grandmother or a brand-new mom. But a woman with a heart for God will have a heart for others and will have a life lived for the Father. You can glean from her and grow.

You can follow Paul's guidelines of who can be an elder in the church as a great way to make sure you're following someone that won't lead you down a wrong path (1 Timothy 3). The last thing you want is a "cool lady" who would rather hang out and tell you what you want to hear, rather than speak truth in love to help you walk in freedom and relationship with Christ. You don't need trendy, you need truth. Pray and ask God to send you a mentor. He believes in the system so He totally will. Maybe she's a youth leader or the children's pastor. Maybe she's the pastor's wife or the worship leader.

She needs to be someone whose life shows her heart for Jesus, not just talks the talk; look for the fruit of her life in the lives of those she's reached. Keep in mind that humility will open doors that stay shut for pride because it very well may begin with seemingly menial assignments like vacuuming or folding bulletins.

What Discipleship Looks Like..

Discipleship looks like growth through relationship. Jesus was with His guys for three years. They did life together and out of life Jesus took the opportunity to teach, train, coach, correct, encourage and challenge these guys into a deeper level of faith. The goal was growth, not friendship. We can have friends but that's different from discipleship. The more they followed, the more He revealed. Those that only followed at a distance got a distant revelation. Those that followed close received a close revelation.

If there isn't anyone around you that will really challenge your growth, pursue it in books and YouTube videos of those who have pressed through in an area, whether it be healing, the prophetic, biblical study etc. Again, follow Christ through people who have established fruit. Jesus will always be your ultimate example.

Discipleship doesn't have some specific formula...sometimes it's over coffee, sometimes it's witnessing together, sometimes it can be working together on a project or reviewing last Sunday's message. Sometimes it's joining in prayer together or being held accountable in an area in which you're growing. Dig into the Word and build your life upon it with someone.

Jesus discipled twelve and by doing so was able to cultivate the gifts that God had already placed in their lives. After He ascended into Heaven, these gifts propelled them into ministry once they answered the call to continue for the cause of Christ. We continue His discipleship in our lives when we respond by growing in the gifts He has already given us.

Spiritual Gifts

I love Christmas and I love giving gifts. After everyone has opened their presents, there is always someone that crawls under the Christmas tree to make sure nothing was left unopened.

God loves giving gifts, too, and way more than we could ever imagine. Sadly, most of us settle for the gifts we have already opened, not going back under the tree for more. Salvation, for example, is a HUGE gift. I am definitely not speaking little of the greatest gift God could have ever given us. But God wanted to give us a lot more than just salvation, so much so, that he underwent far more so that we could experience healing, peace, deliverance, freedom, provision, protection and restoration. The list could go on forever. Yes, salvation, yes! But the Father's gifts are limitless!

Paul lists out several sets of gifts God has given: exhortation, giving, leadership, mercy, prophecy, service, teaching (Romans 12), administration, apostle, discernment, faith, healings, helps, knowledge, miracles, tongues, interpretation of tongues, wisdom (1 Corinthians 12), evangelism, and pastor (Ephesians 4).

It's like that awesome package waiting for you under the Christmas tree and if you leave it there, it becomes a decoration. If the present is never opened, the gift is never enjoyed. Yeah, it's pretty, but it doesn't really do anyone any good to leave an unwrapped gift under the tree. There are more gifts under your Christmas tree, free for the taking, if you'll desire more than what you have now.

Eagerly Desire

From before the creation of man, God foreknew you and called you to walk in the fullness of every gift He poured out. Gifts are available to all in fullness. The most generous God of the Universe didn't sprinkle out His goodness like those Christmases, when there was only enough for one present each. His gifts are abundant and overflowing and continuous. The only limitation is the extent to which we pursue.

Paul tells us to eagerly desire the greatest gifts (1 Corinthians 12:31). This means they are there and waiting for you to go after by faith. It's like the man with the crippled hand, because had he never had the faith to stretch out his hand for Jesus to heal, it would have remained crippled (Matthew 12:13). Your gifts are the same way. If you never reach out in faith to pursue more of what God has for you, your gifts will remain dormant and useless.

I would hate to think that Jesus went through all that extra for nothing (Isaiah 53). But if I settle at salvation, that's the extent of what I am appropriating into my life from all that He did for me.

Like the disciples, maybe we are leaning on the gifts that are already operating in the lives of those around us, so we don't feel the need to step out into what God has for us to do. Jesus had to push his disciples out of the nest a little bit, sending them out of His reach, before He was taken "out of the picture." But He knew one day they'd have to do it on their own, with the Holy Spirit, without Him there to hold their hand. If you're relying on your pastor, will your classmates or co-workers ever see the power of God operate in you? It's one thing to invite them to church, hoping they'll answer the pastor's altar call. It's another thing to bring the church to them and allow the power of God to operate through you. Your world needs you and the gifts God is cultivating in you.

You won't pursue something you don't realize is in your reach. The more you dig into God's Word and realize His heart is in what He wrote, the more you will discover all the amazing gifts He has waiting for you to explore.

He knows that your life will blossom when you are connected intimately to His thoughts towards you and His thoughts towards others through you. Let God love on someone like that through your life and you will thrive being used by God in that way.

Study the Scriptures. Join a Bible study. Go to conferences. Read books. Develop a spiritual gift that connects you to the heart of the Father and then allow Him to connect to others through you. He has tailor made you to have certain strengths. You are especially good at certain things. Don't take this for granted. Pursue them through the eyes of a spiritual gifting and ask that God breathe on your life so you become how He already sees you.

What does all this have to do with being single? Just that, you're single. This means there is love on the inside of you that needs to be shared, for your sake and theirs. Discipleship is a beautiful way to develop our walk with Christ in community through relationship.

You won't pursue something you don't realize is in your reach. The more you dig into God's Word and realize His heart is in what He wrote, the more you will discover all the amazing gifts He has waiting for you to explore.

Go exploring.

"

you have gone into my

FUTURE

to prepare the way.

PSALM 139:5 TPT

Abba,

To get to where I'm wanting to go, the way is in Your Word, so I will take it in and let it become who I am. Your wisdom is my success (Joshua 1:8). Even when I feel trapped by hardship, I will shout Your praises! How else will I know patience, if I never endure? Temper the steel of my virtue in the forges of patience as I keep alert for all You are about to do. Earth cannot contain everything You flood into my life through the Holy Spirit (Romans 5:3-5).

I am brave. I am strong. I refuse to give up because You are near (Psalm 31:24). Fill me with peace and joy and to the brim with hope, pour in resurrection power by the Holy Spirit (Romans 15:13). I depend on Your strength (Psalm 147:11). You are my lifeline and I am holding on to You with all I've got for the promised hope in Your presence (Hebrews 6:19).

Help me to trust You from the depths of my being, not resting any longer on my own ways of doing things. I am desperate to hear You to keep me headed in the right direction. I run from all I was to all that You are (Proverbs 3:5-8). You are the one and only to come through, so I'll wait as long as it takes. All my hope rests in Your embrace. I am secure in You so can now I finally take a deep breath again, I'm safe. I trust You. Absolutely. My lighthouse and refuge from the storm (Psalm 62:5-8).

You are where I am headed until I rest in Your arms,

Daughter

Chapter Eleven: Maturing your Finances

It was the summer before my second year of college that I bought my first home. I was eighteen. Apparently, that's too young to purchase a house, so my dad had to take me to the courthouse to legally declare me as an adult.

It all started when on a normal drive to church I saw a new house that had just been built. My heart fluttered. It was beautiful and just how I'd imagined my first house would look like. It had country yellow accents, a red front door, exposed brick and a large front porch. I called my dad and asked if he thought I could buy a home.

I had already been thinking about moving out but wasn't in a hurry. I was content until my heart began to dream when I saw that house. A few phone calls later, followed by a few days of house shopping and there it was. I was a brand new homeowner. I didn't get the house I saw at first, with the winding driveway and the hardwood floors. I did, however, get a three bedroom cookie-cutter all brick home with a one car garage. It wasn't my dream but it was a perfect fit.

I remember the photo I took in front of the house, though I wouldn't show it to anyone. I had the worst white capris pants on with a weird button up shirt. My hair was way too short and it was just awkward. This awkward eighteen year old just made one of the wisest financial decisions she's made in her whole life! It was either a house or a 350-Z. The house. Much. Better. Choice.

How did I do it? God's favor and elbow grease. I had been working since I was 14. I babysat full time over the summers, started at Domino's pizza by 16, had a handful of other jobs, each growing my skillset and diversifying my experience. I worked full time, part time and went to school full time. I didn't save money. I am a terrible saver. But with each job my dollar per hour was higher and my position a bit more substantial.

No matter what stage of life you're in, you are going to have to deal with money. You will make and spend a ton of money over your lifetime, some more than others. My word of advice: Spend. It. Well. Would my future self be proud of the financial decisions I am making? Would my future-self wish I had saved more or spent more? Would I think I had wasted money or invested it well? It is going to be different for everyone. Maybe you're too frugal and need to have more fun. Maybe you're having way too much fun and need to be more frugal.

Be a Good Steward

Just like everything else in life, you are a steward of your finances. A steward is someone who takes care of something that belongs to someone else. Your money isn't yours, not even wages earned from working (Psalm 24:1). Everything in your life, including your money, is given to you by the grace of God. This gift connects you to His abundant goodness and the rich pleasure of knowing Him in many different ways. If you remember this, you will spend your money in a better way. The better you spend it, the more rewarding that area of your life will be, and the more God can bless you, as you are faithful with what you have.

Generosity is Contagious

No matter how well you spend your money here on earth, once it is gone, it's gone. The only way to make any investment have eternal value is to sow it into the Kingdom of God. The Bible has a lot to say about finances and I think we, as a church, can get so caught up about the tithe, the law and grace that we overcomplicate the simplicity of the Gospel. He is generous. He gives. He sends. He creates. He answers. He provides. We become generous as we become like Him. If you are struggling over tithing 10%, the root issue probably isn't law versus grace, or even money at all, but a heart not yet rooted deeply in trust and relationship. This can be an underlying current that affects every other area of our lives as well. If this is you, I encourage you to open the conversation with God about where your trust may be weak. He desires to see perfect trust produce absolute freedom in you, and all for your benefit.

Dream Huge...

When you read that part, about God blessing you more…please don't say, "I've got enough" or "I'm good with where I am" or "I don't need more." Oh, my goodness, nothing will cap your faith dream more quickly than a complacent attitude! I could make billions and still not have enough because those billions aren't for me, but to funnel through my life into people and ministries and missionaries all across this globe for the sake of the Kingdom. God hasn't entrusted me with billions yet, but every dollar that comes into and out of my bank account is a test of my faith in how big I am dreaming for Him and trusting Him with it.

> The world of the generous gets larger and larger; the world of the stingy gets smaller and smaller. The one who blesses others is abundantly blessed; those who help others are helped." Proverbs 11:24-25 MSG

The tithe is a great place to start, but a terrible place to stay. Build your faith in God for more. The more you are generous, the more God will give you so that you can be even more generous. This isn't greed here. This is changing your perspective from earning and spending your money for yourself and being a steward of finances that has potential for a huge eternal impact on others.

What if you set a goal to be able to financially plant a church in a foreign country, send a missionary to the enslaved and impoverished, start a feeding program in the slums, build an orphanage in a war-torn nation or fund local missions through your own church to reach your city? Dream BIG!

Find a Plan and Stick To It...

There are plenty of resources out there that can help you put a plan together. Find one that works for you and stick with it. It will most likely change as seasons change, but be diligent with what you have now. Don't wait until there's a second income. Don't wait until you make more, or have a car, or a house, retire…. or whatever. If you wait now, you will find another excuse to wait later and then you will wait your whole life. Chances are money will make you miserable and God will not have been able to accomplish the things that could have been funneled through your bank account.

If you would like to dig in a little further, here are just a few scriptures on generosity. I do say a few, because there are over 2,000 of them in the Bible. Whoa!

Leviticus 25:35-37, Psalm 41:1-3, Proverbs 11:24-25, Proverbs 19:17, Proverbs 21:13, Proverbs 22:9, Matthew 10:42, Luke 6:37-38, Luke 21:1-4, 1 Timothy 6:17-19

A few simple ideas to get you thinking:

1. Tithe the 10% and give generously.

This is basic Christianity and simple obedience. All the rest are great, but won't help if this one is out of order.

2. Avoid debt, but if you can't altogether, save it for purchases that will still have value in five years. This will put your purchases into perspective and keep you from impulse buying on credit for things not in your budget. Those shoes are not worth 24.6% interest for the next couple of years, causing you to really spend six times as much for them as the sticker price.

There is a real temptation to use credit cards for flexible spending. I would encourage you not to put anything on a credit card that you can't pay off by the end of that month. This allows you to reap benefits like points, cash back and mileage, but not at the cost of a high percentage rate. If you are not disciplined to pay it off early and often, I would not advise it altogether.

3. If you already have debt, pay it off with a vengeance. This takes real determination, but it will be worth it. Make some sacrifices. Sell some stuff. Move or get a roommate. Take drastic measures to start knocking this mountain down. You'll get there; you just have to keep going.

There are methods to help guide you in this. There is a great resource of teachers, authors and speakers with great biblical wisdom on finances. These are gifts to the body of Christ, but only if we use them!

4. Establish a savings account to cover several months of bills in case of emergency. Unexpected things in life happen and when you aren't prepared, you can spiral backwards. Save and then add to that savings account and don't touch it, unless it is a legitimate emergency. When you do use it, pay your savings account back.

My greatest success in savings came when I opened a savings account at a different bank, with no checks or debit card to it, then auto-deposited a percentage of my check each pay period. Most jobs encourage auto-deposit and allow up to two or three accounts.

5. Find ways to cut spending so you can pay your debt off quicker, build your savings and give more. This is where creativity really plays a role. Eat leftovers. Buy generic. Shop at better value grocery stores.

I rarely buy anything at full price anymore. Most retailers, and even grocery stores, mark up to mark down. So get it on the mark down, sale, special or with a coupon. A little goes a long way if you then take that little and re-route it towards debt, giving or savings.

6. Find creative ways to build wealth. I am crafty so sometimes it's making something and then selling it. You could have a yard sale, write a short story, paint or draw.

Do you have an ability that is a real strength? Just a hint...not everyone can do what you do! So find a way to do it for others as a side gig. Do you design websites, take great photos, apply make-up well, love planning parties, watching children, decorating for the holidays...it's as multi-faceted as there are people, but you've got something special you could share and benefit from at the same time.

7. Look for ways to bless someone that God puts on your heart, without them knowing it was from you. This creates a vacuum

in your life for more and you will be able to pour out in ways you always wanted to but never could because you weren't prepared.

Flowers, notes, cards, gifts…these don't have to cost much, or anything at all, but a little thought and time! Be intentional. Put reminders in your calendar. Don't wait for the inspiration, plan for it!

8. Save up for the fun things like trips, concerts, mission trips and other adventures. Have some goals and shoot for them. Let life be fun and adventurous, but prepare for some of it so it won't always feel like a burden when you get home and have to punch that clock again.

I like to have one trip every year that requires time off from work and a break from my normal routine. Saving up and budgeting for it allows me to relax and enjoy the trip so much more when I'm not counting my pennies and stressing whether or not I'll be able to pay my bills when I get back.

9. Make faith goals for your saving and giving each year so that you can accomplish more than you did the year before. Start where you are and then increase. Maybe you're giving the tithe, but your heart is longing to do more, so don't stop at the 10% because maybe your next faith step is to give 20%. If you save a certain dollar amount out of each check, increase it the same way. Learning to live off less will mean your money will count for more.

I've heard it preached that every time you get a raise, God should too. I love this principle. This means that because I have more coming in, due to a raise, bonus or surprise check in the mail, doesn't mean I become a larger consumer. Yes, enjoy the fruits of your labor, but try not to consume all of the increase.

10. Assign every dollar to a purpose. Any unassigned income will be spent outside of your goals, so know where every dollar is supposed to go and spend/save it there.

Ever put a $20 bill in your wallet only to then wonder where it went? I am guilty times one thousand. Knowing how much is coming in and how much is going out and where to, will help you stay informed of your spending habits. From there you can easily make necessary adjustments as needs arise, seasons change or a dream opportunity comes up.

I love how God gives us tools in every area of our lives to partner with His heart, connect with His mission and increase the enjoyment of our lives. Money is just one of these many tools if we steward it well.

"

leave all your
cares and at the feet
anxieties of the LORD,
& measureless
grace will
STRENGTHEN YOU.

PSALM 55:22 TPT

Abba,

You love me back together again, until all the scattered pieces of my shattered soul are refitted to Your design. Nothing missing or out of place, my life song will be heard by You again. Your brokenness healed me. Your blood washed me. You gave yourself completely so I could be whole again and joined with You (Colossians 1:20, 22). I was lost and unaware of all I had gotten into, but Your holiness drew me into life (1 Peter 1:15-16). I had nothing to do with it. I am cleansed, not just how I now live, but in the hidden reservoirs of my heart. My old life spilled out by repentance and Your new life poured in with restoration (Titus 3:5-8).

Turn things around for me, rebuilding what was lost until I am splendid again. Thankfulness pours out of my life and laughter spills from my heart. My days shaded by depression are past and all is new, even better. Fully living, I run to You with open arms (Jeremiah 30:18-22) because I am back on my feet, this time for good (1 Peter 5:11).

Flourishing with You,

Daughter

Chapter Twelve: Maturing your Relationship with Christ

I opened this book by saying "If you try to avoid being single or rush through it, you'll miss everything God wanted to develop in you through this once-in-a-lifetime part of your journey! There is a purpose for it and it likely won't last forever." This season is the only season where your life is your own. Once you get married, your responsibilities are divided in commitment to your husband, and even more so once you have children.

> "...In the same way, a woman who is no longer married or has never been married can be devoted to the Lord and holy in body and in spirit. But a married woman has to think about her earthly responsibilities and how to please her husband." 1 Corinthians 7:34 NLT

You are only single (not yet married) once. You have your hours, days and years to spend the way you choose. You follow the path you decide. You cultivate your preferences, build your dreams, satisfy your wants and ultimately live for you. This is not a bad thing. This was designed by God, to live this life alone with Him first.

After this season, you don't have the ability to choose for yourself like you can now. If your life is too busy to cultivate and mature your relationship with God, you very well may live an entire lifetime too busy.

I understand your life may be full. School, college, friends, jobs, activities, hobbies, responsibilities...I'm not belittling a full schedule. I've always had one! I want to soberly encourage you to structure your life in this season, so that you are well prepared for every one that is going to follow. This begins and ends in the nearness of your walk with Christ. Period. Nothing will ever be more important.

Every other thing in your life, through every season, will flow from this, because it is what you were made for. You were made to know Him.

Miriam was single when she protected her brother Moses, saving the deliverer of the Israelites. Joseph was single when he interpreted the dreams of the Egyptian king. David was single when he fought and beat the Philistine giant. Jeremiah was single when he received the revelation of how intimately God knew him. Daniel was single when he escaped the jaws of the lions, convincing the king in one night that God was the only true God. John the Baptist was single when he prepared the way for the coming Messiah. Jesus was single when he became the Sacrificial Lamb of God to pay for our sins with his own blood.

There is one unifying and most important theme that ties these great men and women together in the fabric of our history. Yes, they were single but even more so they had a personal relationship with God. This is what gave them the courage and determination to make such history changing choices; to live for something greater than just themselves.

Miriam saved her brother.
Joseph interpreted others dreams.
David fought Israel's battles.
Jeremiah prophesied to a generation.
Daniel's stand for faith brought revival to an entire country.
John the Baptist prepared the way for someone greater.
Jesus sacrificed himself for the sake of all.

Just like these lives and these stories, your life has the potential to accomplish epic things for God. However, it can't happen outside of a relationship with Him, because you won't give your life for someone you do not know, care about or love. Neither will you accomplish the potential that is already in you, as a daughter of God, without knowing Him.

Epic stories of God's chosen started when they chose to respond to the nature of God, as He demonstrated it to each of them in a personal way. God is relational. As a Father, He is pursuing a deep and personal connection with you, His daughter. He's not after a servant to do things for Him. He's after your heart that responds to His. He is not looking to copy and paste someone else's story onto your life. You have your own epic adventure. Take the first step. Take hold of His hand. And begin walking together.

When It's Not Relationship

Say you and your guy have been dating for several months and the relationship is getting serious. You've had a lot of quality time together, some deep conversations, you've met each other's parents and things are going well. Then out of nowhere he disappears. Like he doesn't answer his phone, doesn't return your calls, isn't at home when you go by. You quickly begin to feel equal parts of worry, anger, disappointment and a tad bit stalker. Days go by. Weeks go by. Now it's been several months. He missed your birthday. He didn't come see you graduate. You had a dear family member pass and he wasn't there for you at the funeral. All of this and then he suddenly knocks on your front door and asks for $20!

No, "I'm so sorry..." He didn't try to explain what happened, where he had been, what he had been doing, just asked for the $20. You, in a fit of rage, slam the door – cause NO you are NOT going to give the guy a penny. You've spent these few months completely broken and confused and now he pops back in, unannounced, and is just completely selfish!

But don't we do this very thing to God?

Don't we forget about Him, don't talk to Him, stop going to church, stop obeying His Word, continue with our lives our way. Then our lives go to crap and we need something to ease the pain and make it right again. So we knock on His door because we know He has what we need. But without any repentance or concern for His side, we selfishly ask for something. We need a job, to pass a class, a family member to get out of the hospital, money for an unexpected expense, for a friend to apologize, a parent to see our side, for...the list is endless! And we expect something out of a relationship we have not cultivated. Not only have we not cultivated it, but we have abused it.

God is not your genie in a bottle to give you whatever you want. He wants to give you the world, every good and perfect thing, but for our sake He funnels into our lives through union with Him.

Building this solid foundation takes time. I don't mean to imply that it is going to be forever before you are walking in the cool of the day, knowing the thoughts of the One who first thought of you. I mean it's going to take time out of your busy schedule, away from your social calendar, when you're tired and would rather sleep, when Facebook and Instagram updates are ringing on your phone. It's going to take intentional, planned, purposed time set apart with just you and Him for you to develop an intimacy with the Almighty Creator of the Universe.

Time is a commodity and we all have the same amount. Regardless of intentions, we spend our time on what is most important to us. You will not cultivate a rich relationship with God, if you are not intentional in the time that you spend with Him. Without true heart engagement, it will be superficial, shallow and weak. God cannot prove His power through a vessel that will shatter in the process.

There is no formula. Scripture offers guidelines and examples, such as, David seeking the Lord night and day (Psalm 55:17, Psalm 88:1, 1 Kings 8:59); Daniel praying on a consistent schedule (Daniel 6:10); Jesus often going off by himself to pray (Luke 5:16, Mark 1:35, Matthew 14:23). We see that the greater victories were won by those who lived out of deep dependence. This is a lesson for all of us. We can't expect to go at life alone and accomplish great things on our own without the power of the great One on the inside. This is a partnership forged in togetherness.

After the book of Malachi, there was a period of darkness, division and despair. The voice of God was quiet and infrequently heard among His people. Whose was the voice that broke the silence? John the Baptist. He lived a life of sacrifice and selflessness in order to prepare the Way for Jesus to be heard, received, believed and trusted. John knew his life was not meant to be lived for himself. He was called by God, and John received his calling when he was willing to lay aside personal comfort and cultural pleasures. His desire was to draw near to God and separate himself for the sake of His Kingdom (Luke 1:15, Matthew 3:4).

He was willing to give it all up, and in return, he became the voice of God that broke over 400 years of silence by declaring "prepare the way for the

Lord's coming" (Mark 1:3 NLT). Jesus even referred to him as the greatest of all men.

Do you think it was worth it for him to sacrifice and be different than the crowd and even the other religious people of his day? Absolutely! I'm not saying you'll live a life of singleness like John the Baptist did. Maybe you will. But either way, your investment and sacrifice for the Kingdom will always be well worth it! A deep, rich, intimate, loving, trusting, dependent relationship with God is worth what you'll have to give up in order to cultivate it.

It Takes Devotion

We know it is going to take time but that time must be intentional. This is where purposeful intention meets a personal relationship. God is super important and so is your devotional life with Him. Make an appointment with Him and keep it. Add it to your phone's calendar, set up a reminder, and don't let other events be scheduled during this time. He is worth it. You are worth it. Being intentional may seem forced at first, until your appetite to hunger for the things of God becomes stronger than desire for what you were feeding yourself in the past. If you wait until you "feel" like it, it will probably never happen, or be on an inconsistent basis. Especially while single, prioritize this time and keep it. You'll be glad you did!

Is it in the morning? After dinner? Before or after school? This may not be a time on a clock, but a part of your daily routine. It will also change as seasons in your life change. For example, there will be times when those babies do come along, and that "quiet time" will be rare and much more difficult to maintain. A solid foundation in the Word and relationship with Christ will set you up to thrive even in seasons when your devotional times aren't as consistent or quiet as they can be now.

Find a time that works and keep it. When it changes, be flexible to re-adapt and keep going. If you fall off the boat just get back on. Again, God is more interested in the relationship than you "punching a clock" out of duty. Consistency doesn't mean boring or redundant. If this happens, switch things up and try something new. Just be intentional about it and keep at it.

It Takes Vulnerability

We are able to see into the close nearness that David had with God through his writings in Psalms. We see his highs and lows, his mistakes and grievances, his challenges and victories, his love for God and his unwillingness to waiver in praise to a God who was worthy. David was vulnerable before the Lord and in return God gave him a heart after His own.

To be vulnerable is to be utterly honest, open, hiding nothing and willing to bare all for the sake of transparency. Vulnerability before the Lord sometimes even looks like repentance. David screwed up big time and we remember because it was so scandalous. His life was an example of God's grace because, even though David failed big time, God redeemed him big time. David was humble enough to repent, acknowledge he was wrong and honor God by being honest about what God already knew (2 Samuel 12, Psalm 51). By relationship God restored Him and His Presence continued to rest upon him.

Even Isaiah was brought before the presence of the Lord and his first response to the holiness of God was that he was unclean and tainted (Isaiah 6). We are covered by the grace of God through the shed blood of Jesus Christ, but our lives still bear the influence of the old man when we give way to temptation. Repentance before God clears our conscience and allows us to freely respond to His love and grace, to hear His voice and know His heart. This is where there is no condemnation, because we release the case that the devil would bring against us (Romans 8, Revelation 12:10).

Through vulnerability in our relationship with Christ, we eliminate the position for the enemy to be able to build barriers on our weakness and strongholds in our mistakes.

It Takes Receiving

A near second to the devil, we are our worst critic and a lot of times this keeps us from receiving the love that God is desperately trying to pour into our hearts. We tell ourselves we're not worthy, we're not good enough, we don't do enough, don't respond right, should have said something different, on and on and on. The devil doesn't have to do much fighting, because we beat ourselves up pretty well. This is so defeating in our relationship with God and shouldn't be the case as His daughter.

He doesn't see you the way you see you. He sees you through the blood of His Son which means you are His perfect, whole, completely accepted, loved, adored and beautiful daughter in whom He delights. He doesn't see your flaws, your insecurities, your cellulite, your wrinkles, your acne, your big nose or tall forehead or the shallow areas of your character. He sees you through the eyes of Love.

You have to know Him and know His ardent pursuit of you in order to receive His love, despite all the reasons you think you're not worthy. His choosing you is what makes you worthy.

Go to the "Love Study" with the list of Scriptures on how much God loves you and meditate on them until they tear down every wall you've built between His love and your heart. You are worthy of His love and His love is grand.

Out of everything else that we have competing for our attention, maturing our relationship with Christ should be of upmost importance, especially now. Imagine the epic life that is waiting for you on the other side of saying "I do" to God first, and walking with Him in full surrender. This, this is a beautiful life!

"

your favor wraps around each one &

COVERS

them under your canopy of

kindness and joy.

Abba,

As I get to know You, I unfold all that You've already given me for everything I'll ever need, so I live to know You more and daily accept the invitation to Your love (2 Peter 1:3). Your plan for me is to live whole, beginning now, that's why You gave me Your everything in Jesus (John 3:16). You thought of everything I could ever need and fulfilled it already, for here and all eternity, by Your Son (Psalm 68:9).

If rain is what I need, You send it, blessing all that I produce and the work of my hands. Your provision is always enough so I will not need and borrow, but will be able to give and help others. In You I live from abundance, not lack, from wisdom, not fear (Deuteronomy 28:11-14).

Opening the rocks in the desert, You refreshed Your children; no situation is impossible for You (Psalm 78:15). So I ask for help because You love helping me (James 1:5). Because where You lead, I follow, I have need of nothing. I find rest in trusting You and drinking from Your presence. I have no need to fear making a mistake, because You are with me. You gave me Your Word to guide me. Lift my weary head so I can take in the beauty of Your love as You pursue me. Being with You is my home and where I want to be (Psalm 23).

Your generosity overwhelms me, You take such good care of me (Philippians 4:19).

The object of Your delight (Psalm 5:12),

Daughter

I see you.
I see you sincere. No more cracks. No more scars.
I see you whole. All the scattered pieces brought back home.
I see you loved. By an everlasting love that
floods your heart with peace.
I see you full. Lacking no good thing.
I see you smile. The pleasures of your soul
overflowing and unguarded.
I see you content. Lacking the comparison
that once shaded your value.
I see you standing. Basking in the sun, the
weight on your shoulders now removed.
I see you confident. You have been shown
the way and have walked in it.
I see you pure. The stains of choices past washed by the flood of grace.
I see you rooted. Established in the faith without wavering or doubt.
I see you dancing. Light as air without worry, fear
or care, knowing who has you is able.
I see you trusting. Leaning completely into the
arms of Love with childlike abandonment.
I see you valued. Your worth now settled in the Cross, no compromise.
I see you married. To the man that you were created to match.
I see you living. Life eternal that begins in the now.

Waiting. Maybe the hardest part. Not knowing.
I only see in part, so I have no true answer but that
I only see in part. And in that, there is hope.
Because though I may miss the miracle in the
common, He never misses a moment.
You are so utterly seen and intimately known. Loved and
desired. Ardently pursued. Tenderly cared for. Audaciously
protected. Voice heard, heartfelt, tears gathered. Surrounded
and consumed by His wrap-around Presence.
He sees you. And that is the most important.

Savoring Single

I was on my knees covered in tears. The dozen snotty tissues were evidence of my grief. It was one of those messy moments where God had my heart and I was undone. My dream of being married was my dream. My "finding myself." The one thing that I felt would have made my life better and more complete. I had lived that way for thirty years. Thirty years of pursuing God as an option. I chose Him when I wasn't chosen. I served Him when there was no one else to serve. I loved Him when there was no one else to love. He wasn't my first. He was the benched player that came into the game when there was no one else to fill the spot.

I had given my life to Him but reserved my heart for the love that hadn't yet come along. I sat in church, worshipped, read my Bible, prayed and did all of what we do as Christians. Things that we're told will make us feel better. Make us a better person. To live a better life. But I was still empty. I was void of love. Not because I wasn't loved, but because I couldn't believe it looking at a promise still unfulfilled.

It was in that prayer service that my whole life changed. I gave Him my dream. I finally chose Him first. I chose Him only. I surrendered my true heart to Him and in brokenness and freedom relented. If I never get married, I still choose Him. If my dreams never happen, I still love Him.

This is what it's all about. Is He your first? Is He your only? What if you never get married? What if you never have kids? What if that one dream that's in your heart doesn't happen? Will you still love Him? Will you still pursue Him?

If you've given your life to Him but have reserved your heart for another, I pray you'll surrender it.

He is the only one that can meet the needs of your life.

He is the only one who can fulfill the longings of your soul.

He is the only one who can love you with Agape love that fills.

It's not a father. It's not a boyfriend. It's not a husband. It's Him.

His dreams for you are far more beautiful than you could dream for yourself. His purpose for your life is greater than can be fulfilled aside from Him. His plans for you are for your good. To take care of you. For your future. For your hope. We don't surrender our hearts to be left with despair that leads to nothing. We let go for something far greater!

If this is you, would you sing this with me? A song you likely already know. If not just pray the words.

> "Lord I give you my heart.
> I give you my soul.
> I live for you alone.
> Every breath that I take.
> Every moment I'm awake.
> Lord, have your way in me."
> (Written by Reuben Morgan, 1995)

> I give you my heart. My dreams and aspirations. My love and affection. The tender places I hold dear. The quiet places no one else knows about.
> I give you my soul. My emotional needs and desires. The things I long for. The places that feel empty. The ways I've filled my life with other things.
> I live for you alone. I lay down the things I can't involve you in and desire to be devoted to you in everything my life touches. And if those things that I've set my heart on, if they don't happen I'll still trust you and live for you because I know your love is perfect concerning me.
> Have my every moment. My waking and sleeping. My busy and my rest. Have my messy moments and my ugly moments. My emotional moments and my celebrations. I want to share every moment with you.
> Would you have your way, Lord? Have *your* way. Not my way and the ways I've planned how my life should go, but

your way. Because your way will always turn out better. You see more and have a far better imagination than I could ever dream. I trust that your way is for my good because you love me.

Amen.

I pray that God has breathed life into your soul and revived things that were broken, restored dreams that seemed lost, relit hopes that had faded, healed wounds that ached and has evaporated every thought that counters the way He thinks of you.

You are beautiful. You are special. You are a wonderful part of humanity. You enrich your world. You enhance this journey. The world is ready for you to come out of waiting and embark, with fresh breath and life, in this epic adventure. You are called for purpose. You are chosen for the miraculous. You are sent for love. You are wanted.

> "Don't be wishing you were someplace else with someone else. Where you are right now is God's place for you. Live and obey and love and believe right there. God, not your marital status, defines your life." 1 Corinthians 7:17 MSG

Savoring Single is just this: allowing God to define your life by enjoying where you are right now, in God's place for you. Living, obeying, loving and believing! Open your eyes and take in all the beauty to behold and the wonders of your heart to explore.

In the overwhelming, wrap-around Presence of God you are absolutely loved, wanted, cherished and known. If you ever doubt it, run back to this place where it is always true. His arms spread wide for you, His favorite girl!

In this with you girl,

Shelley Black

Hope of Salvation

If you were to breathe your last breath right now, are you 100% certain, without any doubt, that you would spend eternity in Heaven? If yes, why?

If your answer is anything less than the washing of the blood of Jesus through repentance and total surrender of your life through faith in Jesus Christ, and walking in relationship with Him.

If your yes wasn't that, or if you answered no, you need to get real and face the fact that Heaven is to gain and hell is to lose. Jesus gave His everything and died a real death, on a real cross, then rose from a real grave, so you could walk in real love, through real repentance, by real faith in the real grace of our Lord Jesus Christ!

Your momma can't save you. Your religion can't save you. Your denomination can't save you. Your tip in the offering plate can't save you. Nothing. That means NO THING can save you but the washing of the blood of Jesus. It is available to all but only applied by choice.

It's your choice today. Because tomorrow isn't promised to anyone. A N Y O N E (Proverbs 27:1)!

But you say, "I'm a believer." So is the devil and his demons and they tremble (James 2:19). You must be born again (John 3:3)! But you say, "I'm a good person." Jesus even said why call me good, and He is JESUS (Mark 10:18, Luke 18:19). There is no one truly good. Certainly not good enough to earn your own salvation (Romans 3:10). I pray that as you are reading this, the conviction of the Holy Spirit is revealing this to your heart (John 16:13). Because "all have sinned and fallen short" – yes in all your goodness, you simply are not good enough (Romans 3:23). Because "the wages of sin is death" which means you will, yes die eternally in the pit of hell by inexhaustible flames…but also, bring death to many areas of your life (Romans 6:23).

BUT the "gift of God is eternal life" which means He is the God of second chances and since you are still reading this – there is still hope in perfect redemption and perfect restoration of all you have lost to the wages of sin. He is just that GOOD (Romans 6:23). In the same verse He reveals your judgment, He lays the road to salvation (Romans 6:23).

If you're still reading and are ready to say yes and give your all to Jesus. Pray this prayer, out loud AND with your heart. There is no pastor, altar call or choir required. Just pray in faith and the love of Jesus will fill your heart.

"Dear Lord Jesus, I believe that You are the Son of God and that You died for me. I surrender my life to You. Forgive me of my sin. Wash and cleanse me. Set me free. I believe that You are risen from the dead and that You're coming back again for me. Fill me with the Holy Spirit. Give me a passion for the lost and boldness to preach the Gospel of Jesus Christ. Amen!"

Real faith behind a real confession will render real change that looks like Jesus. Get baptized in water in obedience to Christ (by now just read all of Romans 6).

God loves you. The fulfillment of your every hope and dream is rooted in faith in Him…so start digging!

"Love" Study

The New Strong's Exhaustive Concordance of the Bible, NKJV, by James Strong, LL.D., S.T.D.

Love of God Toward Us

Mark 10:21	Romans 5:5	2 Thessalonians 2:16
Luke 11:42	Romans 5:8	2 Thessalonians 3:5
John 10:17	Romans 8:35	Titus 3:4
John 11:5	Romans 8:37	1 John 2:5
John 11:36	Romans 8:39	1 John 3:1
John 13:1	Romans 9:13	1 John 3:16
John 13:1	2 Corinthians 2:4	1 John 3:17
John 13:23	2 Corinthians 5:14	1 John 4:7
John 14:21	2 Corinthians 13:11	1 John 4:8
John 14:21	2 Corinthians 13:14	1 John 4:9
John 14:23	Galatians 2:20	1 John 4:10
John 15:9	Ephesians 2:4	1 John 4:10
John 16:27	Ephesians 2:4	1 John 4:10
John 17:23	Ephesians 3:19	1 John 4:12
John 17:23	Ephesians 5:2	1 John 4:12
John 17:26	Ephesians 5:2	1 John 4:16
John 19:26	Ephesians 5:25	1 John 4:16
John 20:2	Ephesians 5:25	Jude 21
John 21:7	Ephesians 5:28	Revelation 1:5
John 21:20	Ephesians 6:23	Revelation 3:9
John 3:16	Philippians 2:1	Revelation 3:19
John 5:42	Philippians 2:2	

Love Others

Matthew 5:43	Romans 13:8	Titus 2:4
Matthew 5:44	Romans 13:9	Titus 3:15
Matthew 5:46	Romans 13:10	Hebrews 13:1
Matthew 6:24	2 Corinthians 2:8	James 2:8
Matthew 19:19	2 Corinthians 8:7	1 Peter 1:22
Matthew 22:39	2 Corinthians 11:11	1 Peter 1:22
Mark 12:31	2 Corinthians 12:15	1 Peter 2:17
Mark 12:33	Galatians 5:13	1 Peter 3:8
Luke 6:27	Galatians 5:14	1 John 3:11
Luke 6:32	Ephesians 1:15	1 John 3:14
Luke 6:32	Ephesians 4:2	1 John 3:23
Luke 6:35	Ephesians 5:33	1 John 4:7
John 13:34	Colossians 1:4	1 John 4:11
John 13:34	Colossians 1:8	1 John 4:11
John 13:34	Colossians 2:2	1 John 4:21
John 13:35	Colossians 3:19	1 John 5:2
John 15:12	1 Thessalonians 3:12	1 John 5:3
John 15:12	1 Thessalonians 4:9	2 John 1
John 15:17	1 Thessalonians 4:9	2 John 5
Romans 12:10	Titus 2:4	3 John 1

Our Love for God

Matthew 22:37	John 14:31	James 2:5
Mark 12:30	John 21:15	1 Peter 1:8
Mark 12:33	John 21:16	1 John 2:15
Luke 7:42	John 21:17	1 John 4:19
Luke 10:27	Romans 8:28	1 John 4:19
Luke 16:13	Ephesians 6:24	1 John 4:20
John 8:42	1 Corinthians 2:9	1 John 4:20
John 14:15	1 Corinthians 8:3	1 John 5:2
John 14:23	1 Corinthians 16:22	2 John 6
John 14:28	James 1:12	

Love as a Noun

Matthew 24:12
John 15:10
John 15:10
John 15:13
John 15:9
John 17:26
Romans 12:9
Romans 13:10
Romans 15:30
1 Corinthians 4:21
1 Corinthians 16:24
2 Corinthians 6:6
2 Corinthians 8:24
2 Corinthians 8:8
2 Corinthians 12:15

Galatians 5:6
Galatians 5:22
Ephesians 3:17
Ephesians 4:15
Ephesians 4:16
Philippians 1:9
Philippians 1:17
1 Thessalonians 1:3
1 Thessalonians 5:8
1 Thessalonians 5:13
2 Thessalonians 2:10
1 Timothy 1:14
1 Timothy 6:11
2 Timothy 1:7
2 Timothy 1:13

Philemon 5
Philemon 7
Hebrews 6:10
Hebrews 10:24
1 John 3:18
1 John 4:16
1 John 4:17
1 John 4:18
1 John 4:18
1 John 4:18
2 John 3
Jude 2
Revelation 2:4

Love of Other Things

Matthew 6:5
Matthew 23:6
Mark 12:38
Mark 12:38
Luke 7:47
Luke 11:43
Luke 20:46

John 3:19
John 12:43
John 15:19
Ephesians 1:4
1 Timothy 6:10
2 Timothy 4:8
2 Timothy 4:10

Hebrews 1:9
1 Peter 3:10
2 Peter 2:15
1 John 2:15
1 John 2:15
Revelation 12:11

Free Study Guide

While you were reading this book, did you think of friends that could benefit from the "Savoring Single" message, too? Or maybe you'd just like to dig into a bit deeper! Either way, head over to www.SavoringSingle.com where you'll find a Free Download Study Guide to use individually or in a group.

& Stay Connected

#savoringsingle

@savoringsingle

Photography

All those beautiful photos taken of me were by
Christi Childs of *The Picture People LA*
www.thepicturepeoplela.com

99670972R00100

Made in the USA
Columbia, SC
10 July 2018